Antidumping Industrial Policy

Antidumping Industrial Policy

Legalized Protectionism in the WTO and What to Do about It

Brian Hindley and
Patrick A. Messerlin

The AEI Press

Publisher for the American Enterprise Institute
WASHINGTON, D.C.

1996

The American Enterprise Institute would like to thank the American Express Foundation and the Sasakawa Peace Foundation for support for this project.

Available in the United States from the AEI Press, c/o Publisher Resources, Inc., 1224 Heil Quaker Blvd., P.O. Box 7001, La Vergne, TN 37086-7001. Distributed outside the United States by arrangement with Eurospan, 3 Henrietta Street, London WC2E 8LU England.

Library of Congress Cataloging-in-Publication Data

Hindley, Brian.
    Antidumping industrial policy : legalized protectionism in the WTO and what to do about it / Brian Hindley and Patrick Messerlin.
      p. cm.
   ISBN 0-8447-7046-9 (paper)
    1. Dumping (International trade)   2. Protectionism.   3. World Trade Organization.   I. Messerlin, Patrick A.   II. Title.
HF1425.H56   1996
382'.5—dc20   96-44891
                                            CIP

Printed in the United States of America

ABC 98   1/21/98

Contents

1 ANTIDUMPING AND PROTECTIONISM   1

2 JUSTIFYING ANTIDUMPING?   6
    Fairness   6
    Dumping as Predatory Pricing   18
    Can Antidumping Be Justified?   22
    Origins   23

3 ANTIDUMPING—JEKYLL OR HYDE?   27
    Proportion of Trade Affected by
        Antidumping   28
    Not Stable Law, but Ever-changing
        Regulations   32
    "Privatization" of Antidumping   42
    Mr. Hyde Has Overthrown Dr. Jekyll   51

4 ANTIDUMPING IN THE URUGUAY ROUND   52
    Safeguards and Voluntary Export Restraints   53
    Contingent Protection in the Uruguay Round   55
    Agreement on Antidumping   60
    Outcome of the Round   68

5 WHAT CAN BE DONE?   70
    Reform   70
    Concluding Comment   76

REFERENCES   77

ABOUT THE AUTHORS   81

CONTENTS

LIST OF TABLES

1–1 Prices and Costs Consistent with Dumping of
Widgets in Country *B* by Producers in Country *A* 5
3–1 "Lineage" in EC Antidumping Cases in the
Chemical Industry, 1970–1989 37
3–2 "Who's Who" of Complaining Firms in EC
Antidumping Cases, 1980–1989 44
3–3 Number of Antidumping Cases Initiated and
Terminated by Measures, the United States and the
European Community, 1979–1989 50

Antidumping
Industrial Policy

1
Antidumping and Protectionism

Protectionism gets a poor press these days. Western governments still sometimes want to act in a protectionist way; but they take care to justify their protectionist acts in terms of the public good and to employ arguments that are at least superficially plausible.

The arguments that support antidumping legislation *are* at least superficially plausible. The central question discussed in this book is whether they are anything more than superficially plausible. Is the antidumping drive addressing a real problem, or is it just protectionism in drag?

A related proposition, however, does not need extended discussion: even those who maintain that antidumping measures have a proper role can hardly deny it. It is that antidumping can easily *degenerate* into protectionism.

One factor that leads to degeneration is the difficulty of calculating the magnitudes on which antidumping is based. Antidumping calculations leave a lot of room for error—and if there is room for error, there is room for abuse.

A product is dumped in country *B* if its price in *B* is lower than in its country of origin, *A*; or if its price in *B* is lower than the cost of production in *A*, "plus," in the words of the GATT, quoted more fully below, "a reasonable addition for selling costs and profit." If a *B* industry producing a like product is injured by dumping, the World Trade Organization (WTO) authorizes the govern-

1

ment of *B* to impose an antidumping duty on the dumped product.

Implementing these ostensibly straightforward tests, however, requires decisions on practical questions of great difficulty. The prices at which products are sold, for example, vary with market conditions (to mention only one of many causes of variation): when a product has been sold at different prices, as is typical, which prices in country *A* are to be compared with which prices in country *B*? If costs are calculated, overhead costs and advertising must be taken into account: how should they be allocated between products? What is a "reasonable" addition for selling costs and profit? A product designed for one market may differ from a similar product designed for another: how are the differences to be taken into account when comparing prices or costs? Are symptoms of injury displayed by the *B* industry attributable to dumping or to other causes?

The many problems of this kind would raise difficulties for a national antidumping authority doing its best to conform to the spirit of the WTO. For a national authority less concerned with the spirit of the WTO than with protecting domestic interests against foreign competition, the problems create a field of opportunity in which the alternative least favorable to exporters can always be chosen in order to "prove" that there has been dumping, and so to justify "remedial" duties.

A second pressure promoting the degeneration of antidumping into protectionism lies in the temptations that antidumping sets up for domestic companies. Seventy to 80 percent of antidumping actions in the European Union and in the United States end with the imposition of trade barriers: a proportion of "guilty-as-charged" verdicts matched by few legal or quasi-legal proceedings outside totalitarian states.[1] Laws that give such a good chance

---

1. The actions of the EU and the United States dominate antidump-

of obtaining a hefty legal barrier to imports must tempt domestic producers competing with imports. It would be astonishing if such producers never tried to exploit antidumping law. It would not be surprising if they sometimes succeeded—or even if they succeeded quite often.

Antidumping so easily degenerates into protectionism that it badly needs a respectable rationale: some reassurance that it is not solely protectionist. Supporters of antidumping offer two. One is that antidumping is necessary to prevent exporters from charging prices so low that domestic competitors are driven out of business; dumping, supporters of antidumping say, is a tactic employed by predatory exporters seeking a monopoly in the national market. The other justification is fairness; even if dumping threatens domestic producers with less-than-mortal injury, they should still be protected from such "unfair" foreign competition.

Each of these arguments is superficially plausible, and each gives persons not actively involved in international trade or antidumping a sense that antidumping is a fully justified measure of public policy. Each therefore calls for serious discussion.

Serious discussion, however, means that "dumping" needs more exact definition. According to Article VI(1) of the General Agreement on Tariffs and Trade (GATT), dumping occurs when:

> . . . the price of a product exported from one country to another
>   (a) is less than the comparable price, in the ordinary course of trade, for the like prod-

---

ing. According to Finger (1993, 4), four jurisdictions accounted for more than 95 percent of the 1,558 antidumping actions reported to the GATT between January 1980 and June 1989: the European Union (285), the United States (398), Australia (488), and Canada (318). Despite the large numbers of Australian and Canadian actions, the sheer bulk of the EU and the United States give their actions greater significance for world trade.

              uct when destined for consumption in the exporting country, or,

(b) in the absence of such domestic price, is less than either

    (i) the highest comparable price for the like product for export to any third country in the ordinary course of trade, or

    (ii) the cost of production of the product in the country of origin plus a reasonable addition for selling costs and profit.

Under Article VI(1)(a) and Article VI(1)(b)(i), dumping occurs when an exporter sells at a lower price in the market of an importing country than in his home market or in a third-country market. But dumping also occurs, according to Article VI(1)(b)(ii), when exports are sold at a price lower than their average cost of production, plus a reasonable addition for selling costs and profit.

The existence of one kind of dumping does not imply the existence of the other (though they are mutually consistent, as when sales are below the cost of production in all markets, but at a greater discount in foreign markets). Each kind therefore requires separate treatment.

To illustrate the different kinds of dumping, table 1–1 gives hypothetical prices and costs of production for a product—call it a widget. Prices are all taken at the factory gate in A, and are net of transport costs, insurance, local taxes, and so forth. For simplicity, unit costs are assumed constant.

The numbers in table 1–1 are assumed to be known with certainty by everyone concerned. Biased calculation of the magnitudes on which antidumping is based is in many eyes the central issue in current antidumping practice, and it is discussed below. In seeking a rationale for antidumping action, though, it is best to assume that the numbers on which the action is based are free from error

TABLE 1–1
PRICES AND COSTS CONSISTENT WITH DUMPING OF WIDGETS IN
COUNTRY B BY PRODUCERS IN COUNTRY A
(U.S. dollars)

Case	Cost of Production in A	Price of Product in A	Price of Product in B
I	100	500	200
II	100	50	50

SOURCE: Authors.

or manipulation. Mistaken or abusive application of a policy does not imply that the policy lacks sound underlying justification. Such justification is therefore more easily approached by abstracting from abuse or error.

Case I in table 1–1 is an example of differential-price dumping by the producer(s) from country A in country B: the price of widgets is higher in A, the country of export, than in B. Case II illustrates below-average-cost-of-production dumping in country B: the price of widgets is the same in A as in B, but below the cost of production in A.

Each case, therefore, passes the first test for WTO-authorized antidumping action by the government of B: there is dumping.[2] The problem is to define the sense in which these configurations of prices and costs might be thought unfair, or to reveal predatory pricing by the A producer(s), or to reveal any circumstances that make exports of widgets from country A a legitimate target of antidumping action by the government of B.

---

2. A second test concerns injury caused by dumping. It is discussed in due course.

2
Justifying Antidumping?

"Fairness" is a tricky ground on which to defend an economic policy. Supporters of a policy will prefer to argue that it will in fact improve the position of those it seems to damage. When fairness is to the fore, that is probably because no other argument is available; and that suggests that those who appear to be hurt by a proposed rectification of the alleged unfairness will in fact *be* hurt.

Predatory dumping, for example, could be described as unfair. But action to combat predatory dumping can also be represented as advantageous for those it seems to injure. Antidumping seems to harm buyers of the allegedly dumped good, who are prevented from buying the low-price merchandise on offer. But if the low price drives other sellers out of business, and the dumper becomes a monopolist, buyers will face higher prices in the future. If buyers properly assess the consequences of antidumping, it can therefore be argued, they will opt for antidumping rather than low current prices. Predatory dumping could be described as unfair, but does not need to be—an ostensibly more compelling argument is available.

Fairness

Despite this difficulty, the slipperiness and subjectivity that characterize notions of fairness can work to the advantage of protectionists. Voters with only half a mind on an issue sometimes too easily concede that fairness demands protection of some domestic interest, even though

6

weaker but morally more defensible foreign interests are harmed thereby. Were these voters to inspect the issues more closely, concern with fairness might suggest a different response.

Anyone wishing to *be* fair will bear in mind the slipperiness and subjectivity of ideas of fairness, especially when fellow citizens call for action to restore fair play that they allege has been disrupted by the tactics of foreigners. Patriotic or nationalistic sentiment plays a role in discussion of fair trade and fair-trade remedies. Nevertheless, the remedies harm fellow citizens as well as foreigners—and typically harm fellow citizens most. Any fairness that antidumping duties might restore to domestic producers is purchased by an increase in the price that domestic buyers must pay for the "unfairly traded" product.

No explicit definition of fairness is offered here. Instead, the simple numbers of table 1–1 are used as the basis for discussion of the effects of dumping and antidumping. The results are then used to ask what concept of fairness, if any, could be invoked to describe the initial state as unfair, or to defend the transition from states brought about by dumping to those created by antidumping.

Differential-Price Dumping. At first sight, it is buyers who face unfairness in case I of table 1–1, especially buyers in the country of export, *A*. The case is consistent with a WTO-legal right of the government of *B* to take antidumping action, but it does not seem that such action would be helpful. Antidumping will push up widget prices in *B*, whereas it seems clear that a sensible *B* policy would aim to get prices down.

The picture, however, does not yet contain any producer of widgets in country *B*. How would their presence affect assessments of fairness and appropriate policy?

The most relevant characteristic of *B* producers, in this context, is their cost of production. Yet whatever the level of those constant costs, no patent unfairness appears. If the costs of production of widgets in country *B* are lower than the $200 selling price in *B* of exports from *A*, the *B* producers are making profits—possibly substantial profits. Those profits would be even higher, of course, if the *B* government took antidumping action and raised the price in *B* of exports from *A*. But to describe as unfair an *A* export price that is higher than *B* costs of production seems to require an eccentric definition of fairness.

If costs in *B* are higher than the $200 selling price in *B* of widgets from *A*, however, the *B* producers clearly have a problem. Unless they can get their costs down, they are likely to be driven out of business, in the absence of anti-dumping action or some alternative form of assistance or protection. Even so, there is no obvious unfairness. It will certainly seem unfair to some that high-cost producers can be driven out of markets by low-cost producers. That process, though, is crucial to the effective functioning of a market economy. And if it is accepted that low-cost domestic producers should be permitted to drive high-cost domestic producers out of business, it is difficult to find respectable grounds for describing the same process as unfair merely because the low-cost sellers are foreign.[1]

Differential-price dumping and market structure. The figures in table 1–1, though, leave economic issues hanging. If *B* producers can make a widget for less than $500, for example, why do they not sell in the *A* market?

One possible reason for a failure of *B* widgets to appear in *A* is that imports into *A* are impeded by one means or another. The *A* market may be heavily protected against imports by tariffs or quotas, or by nontariff barriers such as health and safety standards, or by informal barriers erected by cartels in *A*, which might or might not be

---

1. National security may provide a reason to maintain uneconomic domestic production of some goods. The WTO offers many legal ways of doing that, however. It is not a ground for defense of antidumping.

supported or acquiesced in by the government of A. The A producer or producers might have a "sanctuary market" in A—so that A producers can compete in the B market, but B producers cannot enter the A market. Thus, A producers can make high profits in A, which they can use to attack the B producers in their home market.

That seems unfair. But it is the sanctuary market that is the cause of the unfairness—not the dumping, which is merely a consequence of it. The issue is taken up again in chapter 5.

A sanctuary market in country A, however, is not sufficient to explain the configuration of costs and prices in case I. In particular, it is not enough to explain prices far above costs, or sustained price differences between markets, neither of which could survive competition between widget sellers in A.

A sanctuary market in A *and* a monopoly producer in A, though, could generate numbers such as those of case I. Such a monopolist, secure in his home market, but subject to at least some competition in the world at large (there is at least one B producer), might very well find it in his interest to charge higher prices in A than in B. This is the standard textbook case of a discriminating monopolist.

Dumping and antidumping in oligopolistic industries have been extensively studied (for example, by Brander and Krugman 1983; Prusa 1992; and Anderson et al. 1995). That literature reveals a complex picture, in which antidumping becomes an instrument in the rivalry between the oligopolists, but, in terms of fairness, it does not add anything to what has already been said.

In the present context, a more important question is whether differential-price dumping is conceivable in an industry with many firms. If it is not, a case emerges that action against differential price dumping should be restricted to industries with small numbers of producers at the global level.

In an industry with a large number of firms, a high-price sale will typically yield higher profits for a seller than a sale at a lower price. If widget prices are higher in country A than in country B, competing widget producers in A will want to sell in high-price A rather than low-price B; and competition between them will push prices in A close to costs of production and eliminate price differences between A and B. A member of a multifirm A industry might charge different prices in A and B as a result of error, or because the quality of its product is known in one market but not in the other. Such "dumping," though, does not seem to raise any issue of fairness, and in any event, in its nature, will eventually disappear.

Only one hypothesis seems able to explain persistent differential-price dumping in an industry with many firms. It is that producers in an industry might face some agreed or conventional price in their own country, and will not sell there for less than that price. All production in excess of demand at that price is therefore sold abroad, for whatever the sellers can get, which will typically be a dumping price.[2]

Such a cartel in A will, according to Hindley (1991, 37–38), probably:

---

2. According to Jacob Viner, antidumping duties first appeared as a response to dumping by U.S. cartels of the excess supplies created by their price-fixing activities in the markets of neighboring countries. Canada adopted such an antidumping law in 1904, New Zealand in 1905, and Australia in 1906. Viner (1923, 97) comments that:

Although the prevalence of dumping in the export trade of the United States is not to be explained by the existence of absolute monopoly control in many industries, it is to be attributed in large part to the absence of keen price competition in the domestic market for manufactured and other products produced under large scale conditions. Whether this absence of keen price competition is due to tacit or concealed price agreements, or to interlocking directorates, or to the dominance in the respective industries of single great concerns whose domestic price lists are accepted with or without an understanding of some sort as the

(a) increase *A* exports of widgets, the exports being sold at a lower price in *B* than in *A*; and

(b) increase fluctuations of widget prices in *B*.

Clearly widget *producers* in *B* will not think this fair. Widget *buyers* in *B*, though, will gain, at least initially.[3] To assess fairness, it therefore seems necessary to compare the losses of producers and the gains of buyers. In monetary terms, the gains of buyers are likely to exceed the losses of producers; and the losses that antidumping duties would impose on buyers are likely to be greater than the gains they would provide to producers. An objective observer might nevertheless regard this situation as unfair, especially to *B* producers who entered the market before formation of the cartel in *A* could have been foreseen.

Viner's hypothesis may be an important explanation of dumping at the start of the twentieth century. Today, however, active antitrust policies make it more likely that numbers such as those in case I derive from the existence of a sanctuary market in country *A* combined with few producers in either market. Current antidumping laws, however, can be applied in a vastly broader range of circumstance.

Price-Less-than-Average-Cost Dumping. Price-less-than-average-cost dumping, illustrated by the numbers in case II of table 1–1, is consistent with predatory pricing. It is also consistent with other, less threatening, explanations.

Excess capacity. One explanation for sales at a price less than the average cost of production is excess capacity.

---

standard to be adhered to in all industries, is not material to the present study.

3. "At least initially" because in the longer run, the cartel's activities might wipe out the *B* widget industry even though not designed to have that effect. In that event, the cartel, perceiving the vacuum that its actions have created, might extend its operations to *B*— "predatory pricing" by accident, so to speak.

Indeed, excess capacity can be *defined* as a situation in which all or most firms in an industry are forced by competition to sell at prices less than their average total cost of production.

When excess supply affects an industry in which competition is global, price-less-than-average-cost dumping may appear. Firms located in country *A* and firms located in country *B* may face the same circumstances, and may respond to them in the same way, by cutting selling prices below their average cost of production. But the government of *B* will then be able to identify exports from *A* to *B* as "dumped."

The idea of fairness that might support that legal possibility is hard to define. In the absence of antidumping action, producers everywhere face the same conditions. Excess capacity makes those conditions hard, but there is no evident *unfairness* in the position of *B* producers.

Antidumping action by the government of *B* will allow the prices and profits of the *B* industry to rise if *B* is a net importer of widgets, thus redistributing income from widget buyers in *B* to widget producers in *B*, and further depressing the widget industry in *A*. Widget producers in *B* may congratulate themselves on that outcome. But it is hard to see how it might be described as more *fair* than the outcome without antidumping action.

Can it be made fair by adding more circumstance? The global excess capacity, for example, might be entirely due to poor decisions in *A*—caused solely by ill-judged investments in widget-producing plant and equipment by producers in country *A*. Might it not then be fair to protect the innocent *B* producers from the consequences of the bad decisions in *A*?

Perhaps it would (though the standard of fairness that would require buyers in *B* to finance the protection is not obvious). But, as antidumping law stands, exports from *A* to *B* could be identified as dumped even if the mistakes that created the excess capacity were all made in country *B*. The location of the errors that created the excess capacity may be significant for identification of fairness, but antidumping law does not reflect that.

Different employment practices. A contentious issue associated with excess capacity derives from the existence of different employment practices in different countries. Companies and workers in the United States negotiate contracts that fix wages, but allow firms to hire and lay off workers according to current demand for output. For U.S. firms, therefore, labor cost is a primary determinant of marginal cost. In contrast, it is said, companies in Japan offer workers employment for life, do not lay off workers in times of recession, and therefore treat labor as a fixed cost, having no effect on marginal cost.

Hence, in times of slack demand, all firms push their prices toward marginal cost, but Japanese firms feel able to reduce their selling prices by more than U.S. firms and to maintain their output at a higher level. As a consequence, Japanese output fluctuates less, and U.S. output and employment more, than if firms and workers in Japan adopted U.S.-style labor contracts.

It is easy to see that the price-less-than-average-cost dumping that potentially accompanies this outcome might be described as unfair. It is instructive to ask, though, whether the alleged Japanese employment practices would be regarded as unfair if they were adopted by U.S. firms. If enough firms in a U.S. industry employed workers on "Japanese-type contracts," the effect on the remaining firms in the industry would be the same as that said to arise through trade between the United States and Japan. If U.S. firms and workers freely chose "Japanese" contracts, however, could it reasonably be said that firms or workers adopting them were acting unfairly? If not, what makes it unfair when Japanese firms and workers adopt them?

Start-up costs. Another innocent explanation for price-

13

less-than-average-cost dumping is that in many industries, start-up costs are high. Personnel must be trained and equipment run in. These conditions are perfectly compatible with competition, but if they occur in a competitive industry, new entrants will be obliged to sell at the competitive price, and will therefore initially suffer losses.

A new entrant *exporting* in its start-up phase, however, will be dumping, under the price-less-than-average-cost definition of dumping. There is no evident unfairness in such sales, and no obvious public interest in barring them. But antidumping law permits them to be identified as "dumped."

If domestic firms are legally able to do something—such as selling at a price less than start-up cost—fairness seems to demand that foreign firms should be allowed the same freedom. If antidumping law is based on a concept of fairness, though, it is not *that* concept.

"Dumping" in Domestic Law. Neither in the European Union nor the United States is it per se illegal for a domestic seller to charge different prices to different buyers, or to sell at a price below cost of production.

Bronckers (1995, 80) summarizes the EU position:

> Pursuant to EC competition law, companies are generally allowed to sell at any price they see fit, including below-cost prices. By way of exception, a smaller group of companies holding a dominant position is held to a more stringent predatory pricing standard. As a matter of principle, these companies may not sell below variable costs; and they are not allowed to sell at higher— but still loss-making—prices with the intent to eliminate competitors. Yet, depending on circumstances, even these dominant companies can sell at a considerable loss, for instance in order to align their prices with competitors who threaten to steal away their customers.

Palmeter (1995, 44) describes the broadly similar U.S. position:

> It may indeed be illegal for a domestic seller to discriminate in price between purchasers, but only if it is found to be injurious to competition. The Supreme Court has held that competition may be injured only if the discrimination is predatory, and if it has a reasonable chance of succeeding. . . .

Is Dumping Unfair? Dumping is not intrinsically unfair. Instances of dumping, or circumstances surrounding it, have been identified that might be deemed unfair by a dispassionate observer: for example, sanctuary markets, or dumping of a cartel's excess supplies. But in other instances, dumping can be described as unfair only on an eccentric or biased definition of fairness.

Some dumping may be unfair in some value system. Some dumping, however, will be fair in any acceptable value system. But the WTO and national antidumping laws allow action in both cases. Neither discriminates between "fair" and "unfair."

Injury Conditions for Antidumping. Before the Uruguay Round, the GATT did not condemn dumping per se. The preamble of the Tokyo Round Anti-Dumping Code (Gatt 1979), for example, says that: ". . . *antidumping practices* should not constitute an unjustifiable impediment to international trade . . ." (emphasis added). Only after *that* threat is identified does the preamble go on to say that ". . . antidumping duties may be applied against dumping *only* if such dumping causes or threatens material injury to an established industry in the territory of a contracting party or materially retards the establishment of an industry" (emphasis added).

The Uruguay Round *Agreement on Implementation of Article VI* dispenses with a preamble, but it still requires a

15

demonstration that dumping caused injury: "It must be demonstrated that the dumped imports are, through the effects of dumping . . . causing injury within the meaning of this Agreement" (Article 3.5). Demonstration of dumping, therefore, is not sufficient to warrant WTO-consistent antidumping action. This second condition, however, does not affect the outcome of the discussion above. The causation-of-injury requirement is in fact a very weak constraint on antidumping.

In large part, that is because it fails to separate the factual question of whether an industry has been injured from the very different question of what has caused that injury. The failure is understandable: in legal terms, the separation is difficult to make. In one sense, dumping of a product will always injure the domestic producers of like products. Had the imports been offered at a higher price, domestic competitors would have been able to sell more, or to sell at a higher price. That thought, though, points to the conclusion that if dumping is demonstrated, and the domestic industry displays symptoms of injury, then at least some of the injury must be attributable to the dumping—and the requirement that dumping must be *shown* to have *caused* injury is at risk of vanishing. That is a risk the WTO must guard against if the injury requirement is to be effective.

Symptoms of injury. Before dumping can be shown to have *caused* injury, the industry in question must be shown to display symptoms of injury. The Uruguay Round agreement says that "the examination of the impact [of sales of the dumped products] on the industry concerned shall include an evaluation of all relevant economic factors and indices having a bearing on the state of the industry. . . ." It lists fifteen such factors,[4] several of which include "po-

---

4. "The magnitude of the margin of dumping" is a curious addition of the Uruguay Round to the list of indicators of injury. The addition confounds the two formerly separate elements of dumping and injury.

tential" effects, such as "an actual and potential decline in sales"; but it gives no indication of the weights to be placed upon them, and it cautions that "this list is not exhaustive, nor can one or several of these factors necessarily give decisive guidance." National antidumping authorities therefore have a great deal of scope for deciding that injury has occurred. Any industry not at the height of a boom is likely to display at least some of the fifteen symptoms listed. That it displays symptoms, however, says nothing about what has caused them.

Causation of injury. Causation is difficult to establish. Facts can in principle be observed; but the causal relation between facts, if it exists, cannot be observed.

That dumping has occurred can in principle be demonstrated. That a domestic industry displays symptoms of injury can in principle be demonstrated. But those observations together do not demonstrate that the dumping has caused the injury. There will typically be alternative hypotheses about the cause of symptoms of injury displayed by the domestic industry: for example, that the products of the industry are not attractive, or that a too-high price is charged for them, or that reliable servicing is not provided. Sometimes, evidence persuasively refuting some of these alternative hypotheses will be available. But that cannot be expected as a matter of course.

The force of the requirement that dumping be shown to have *caused* the symptoms of injury of the domestic industry therefore crucially depends on where the burden of proof lies. An antidumping authority will have difficulty in conclusively showing that dumping caused the injuries displayed by the domestic industry. Were authorities required to do so, the causation-of-injury condition would

---

It appears to make a high dumping margin alone sufficient for a determination that the domestic industry has been injured by dumped imports. If so, it even further reduces the constraint represented by the causation-of-injury requirement.

provide alleged dumpers with a strong ground for defense against antidumping action.

Similarly, alleged dumpers will find it hard to show beyond reasonable doubt that their dumping did *not* cause or contribute to the injuries of the domestic industry. If the burden of proof lies with them, the causation requirement provides little ground for defense against charges of dumping and only a feeble barrier to WTO-consistent antidumping action.

The words of the WTO agreement seem to place the burden of proof with the authorities. In reality, though, importers charged with selling dumped goods are likely to find that it lies with them: they must show that the dumping did not cause the injuries displayed.

That is a difficult task, but it need not be insurmountable. It might be possible to show, for example, that dumping did not cause all the injuries of the domestic industry. But when the European Court of Justice, for example, rules that an importer might be deemed responsible ". . . for injury caused by dumping even if the losses due to the dumping are merely part of a more extensive injury attributable to other factors,"[5] it comes very close to removing any barrier that an injury test might pose to antidumping. If alleged dumpers must show that the dumping has not even *contributed* to the symptoms of injury of the domestic industry, the ground for defense provided by the causation requirement is very small indeed. If "dumping" and "injury" have both been shown, and national authorities have only to show that the dumping *contributed* to the injury, they have an easy task, and the causation-of-injury test is irrelevant.

Dumping as Predatory Pricing

Debate about predatory pricing focuses on the logical question of whether there are circumstances in which one

---

5. Canon v. Council, joined cases 277/85 and 300/85 (1988) ECR 5731, para 62. Palmeter (1995, 60–63) provides a lively discussion of the similar position in the United States.

competitor could expect to increase its net worth by charging prices so low that other competitors are forced to exit the industry; and on the empirical question of how actual examples might be identified. This debate takes place almost entirely in the context of domestic competition laws.[6] If predatory tactics are granted some plausibility, however, it is natural to suppose that it might be used across international borders.

The idea of predatory pricing, though, provides only a weak basis for antidumping. One weakness lies in the obvious fact that price wars are expensive for predators. Intended prey can adjust their output to make the best of the low price: predators, to keep the price low, must supply all the demand that the prey do not supply at that price. On standard definitions of predatory pricing, that price will be less than marginal cost, so the predator's losses increase with each unit sold.

The prey all know that prices must rise in the future, so they have an incentive to curtail current output but to stay in the market. Predator and prey will usually be better off if one purchases the other, or if they collude with one another over prices.

Even if the predator succeeds in driving competitors out of production, the size of the gain won thereby is open to question. If the predator is trying to maximize its net worth, it must expect to recoup the losses from its price cutting once it has a monopoly. But it must face the possibility that competitors will reenter the industry when prices rise, or that new firms will enter, and thereby make

---

6. For example, on tests for whether pricing *is* predatory, the Areeda-Turner test (Areeda and Turner 1975) has been accepted by U.S. courts in several antitrust cases. It holds that pricing below short-run marginal cost should be unlawful, and that short-run marginal cost can be approximated by short-run variable cost. It has, however, been the subject of cogent academic criticism (Joskow and Klevorick 1979). No such discussion occurs in the antidumping literature—perhaps because it would expose the hollowness of the pretense that antidumping can be justified by the possibility of predatory pricing.

it difficult or impossible to recoup the losses incurred in the low-price period.[7]

Analysis based on these lines of thought (McGee 1958, 1980) has led to assertions that a rational firm will never use predatory pricing. On this view, accusations of predatory pricing—and therefore of predatory dumping—are always wrong. And indeed, examples of predatory pricing that will stand up to objective analysis have proved difficult to find. Intensive efforts by scholars have yielded a handful of possible examples, stretching back over a century or more (in contrast with 1,558 antidumping cases recorded between 1980 and 1989).

But although plausible examples of predatory pricing are few, they are not zero. Furthermore, recent theoretical analysis suggests that the proposition that predatory pricing will *never* occur may be too strong (Tirole 1988, chapter 9, gives a concise review of the current theory of predatory pricing and related topics).

Moreover, the domestic competition laws in the United States and the European Union both provide for regulation of predatory pricing; and if provisions allowing

7. Entry may not occur, of course, if there are natural barriers to entry in the industry, such as continually decreasing costs. Such industries are not common, though. Moreover, when production technology is such that the industry will naturally be dominated by one firm, the initial predatory-pricing hypothesis comes into doubt. In the first place, it is not needed: by definition, the final survivor will force competitors out of business by one means or another. In the second place, for many purposes, the means by which the final survivor reaches that position is not crucial—if the industry will inevitably be dominated by a single firm, the question of *which* firm is likely to be a secondary consideration in the domestic context.

In the international context, of course, the question of whether the final survivor is foreign or domestic may be of greater concern, and antidumping is a possible means—one among many—of influencing the outcome. To justify antidumping on the ground that it might be a useful means of assisting a national champion to final victory, however, is to concede a very much more aggressive purpose for antidumping than is admitted to by any standard justification.

regulation of the predatory tactics of *domestic* rivals seem useful, it is natural to think that provisions regulating the predatory tactics of *foreign* sellers would also be useful. That leaves open the question, however, of why the provisions for alleged foreign predators should differ from those for alleged domestic predators.

Does Predatory Pricing Justify Antidumping? Predatory pricing does not justify antidumping. A compelling ground for rejection of the proposition that it does lies in the sheer number of antidumping actions, and the diversity of their targets. The possibility of predatory pricing can be used to defend the actual practice of national antidumping authorities only by adopting the absurd position that they must act against *any* behavior that *might* have a predatory intent or effect, however remote the possibility.

Such widespread action will deter predatory dumping. But that antidumping deters predation is not a cogent defense of antidumping. A policy of rigging automobiles to explode if touched by someone other than their owner would probably deter auto theft. In both cases, though, the deterrence itself is costly—almost certainly more costly than the problem it purports to solve.

Most antidumping cases involve products with a considerable number of producers at the global level, none of whom has a dominant share of global output. In such an industry, predatory pricing is inconceivable. In an industry with, say, ten producers, the largest of whom has 20 percent of the market, one producer could achieve only its own bankruptcy by attempting to drive the others out of the market by charging prices lower than marginal cost. In an industry with such a structure, the possibility that predatory pricing will be employed can safely be neglected.

In an industry that consists of two firms, however, the possibility that one of them will engage in predatory pricing cannot be rejected with complete confidence. In such an industry, the possibility of predatory pricing can supply the first step of an economic rationale for antidumping (the second and more demanding step being to show that antidumping is the best means of dealing with predatory dumping).

Can Antidumping Be Justified?

Predatory pricing may be able to supply *a* rationale for antidumping. But it cannot be *the* rationale—it cannot explain the bulk of actual antidumping cases, which involve the dumping of products produced by many firms. If predatory pricing is *the* rationale for antidumping, there is no warrant for authorizing antidumping actions against imports of products produced by many firms, and WTO authorization of antidumping should be limited to industries in which predatory pricing is conceivable—to cases in which few producers compete at the global level.

Of course, to make that proposal effective, the phrase "few producers competing at the global level" requires definition. That is a technical matter, though not an easy or straightforward one, as the extended arguments over market definition in antitrust cases suggest. Wherever a sensible line is drawn, however, it will eliminate large numbers of antidumping cases that are enthusiastically pursued under present law.

Neither fairness nor the possibility of predatory dumping provides a satisfactory rationale for current antidumping law. Both may provide a justification for some action against dumping, but neither can justify the broad scope of the authorization of antidumping action by the WTO, or the broad scope of national antidumping laws.

The circumstances in which predatory dumping might conceivably occur are so restrictive that the hypothesis can account only for a tiny fraction, if any, of actual antidumping cases. Those circumstances, moreover, are easily defined in terms of readily observable magnitudes (a global industry containing only a small number of firms, for example), so that there is no real difficulty in drafting a law that allows possible predatory dumping to be targeted while excluding cases in which predatory dumping is inconceivable.

Unfairness is less amenable to clear legislation—the concept itself is too vague. Current antidumping laws, however, authorize action in many circumstances in which examination fails to yield unfairness (and in which predatory dumping is inconceivable). If the vagueness of "fair" makes translation into legislation more difficult than with predatory pricing, it does not affect the principle. To create an antidumping law that could be defended in terms of fairness, it would be necessary to draft a law that openly defined "unfair"; and then to write into it conditions that ensure that *only* cases of unfair dumping were vulnerable to its sanctions. Even before the question of whether the remedies of current antidumping law provide the best means of dealing with the remaining practices is addressed, that would require major amendment of current laws.

Origins

That neither fairness nor predation can provide current antidumping law or policy with a satisfactory rationale raises a puzzle. If antidumping law has no satisfactory rationale, how did it become so firmly embedded in the legal structure of the world trading system?

A Heritage from Competition Law. The first law to deal with dumping derived from the Sherman Antitrust Act of 1890, the main U.S. law against predatory pricing in the United States by sellers located in the United States. The Sherman Act paved the way for other laws, designed to combat predatory pricing in the United States by sellers not located in the United States. Section 73 of the Wilson

Tariff Act of 1894, for example, developed the provisions of section 2 of the Sherman Act, and authorized fines for firms found to dump and imprisonment for their managers, but it did not authorize duties to offset dumping. The risk that antidumping action might be used as a means of aligning exporters' prices with domestic prices—that is, that antidumping might be used for protectionist purposes—was thereby reduced.

Similarly, the Australian Industries Preservation Act of 1906 was aimed mainly at limiting the exercise of monopoly power by foreign firms. The protectionist potential of the act was defused by requiring, as a condition of application, a demonstration that the Australian industry producing a like product was reasonably efficient, and that preservation of it would be advantageous to the Commonwealth. Other texts—the New Zealand antidumping provisions of 1905; sections 800–801 of the U.S. Revenue Act of 1916; and section 316 of the U.S. Fordney-Mc-Cumber Tariff act of 1922—took the same approach (Viner 1923, chapters XI and XIII).

These antidumping regulations share a common characteristic. It is that they have given rise to very few antidumping actions.

Defusing Protectionist Pressure. Another group of antidumping laws, however, took the Canadian law of 1904 as a model. They made no reference to competition law, and they defined dumping as occurring when exporters charged a higher price in their home market than in the export market. They also defined the home-market price as "the fair market value of the same article when sold for home consumption in the usual and ordinary course." Half a century later, these definitions were embodied in the GATT.

The protectionist potential of this second group of antidumping laws is much greater than that of the first group, based on competition law. If dumping is defined merely as a price difference, with no account taken of market behavior and intent, dumping becomes an arithmetical inequality to be nullified by an antidumping duty levied at the border. Protectionist use of antidumping regulations becomes almost inevitable.

This reflects the typical origin of members of this second group—as attempts to *defuse* protectionist pressures. Governments using antidumping laws for this purpose knew they were offering a form of protection. They hoped, however, that they could control antidumping more closely than they could other protective devices.

The Canadian antidumping legislation of 1904 is an example. The Liberal Party had won votes by pledging protection. When elected, however, it sought a compromise between its traditional free-trade position and the electoral promises it had just made (Viner 1931, 193). Adding antidumping duties to regular tariffs "when necessary" looked like a clever way to do this. The same political and economic backgrounds and the same hope of using antidumping to defuse protectionist pressures lay behind other antidumping laws tabled or adopted in the early twentieth century—for example, the French Law of 1908 and the British Safeguarding of Industries Act of 1921.

Slaloming between opposing trade interests was a feasible tactic for governments formed from parties with strong free-trade wings. In these cases, the protectionist potential of the antidumping regulations was offset by the arcane nature of the enforcement procedures. The British Act, for instance, introduced no less than nine procedural stages. This complexity "blunted the effectiveness of the [British] Act from the outset and there is the suspicion that the then coalition government (which included the free-trading Liberals) deliberately put administrative obstacles in the way of its operation" (Dale 1980, 13). If that was the intention, it was successful—the antidumping provisions of the British Act were never used prior to their repeal in 1957.

Antidumping laws were therefore introduced either with well-defined objectives in view (those based on competition law) or as what was perceived as the lesser of two evils: antidumping, rather than open protectionism. The latter choice might have been the best available at the time. Current problems, though, stem entirely from it. Antidumping may have been under control at first, but, if so, it subsequently slipped its leash.

3
Antidumping—Jekyll or Hyde?

For those who hold that antidumping action is a fully justified measure of public policy, the protectionist content of antidumping is a side effect no doubt regrettable, but impossible to avoid in an imperfect world and without serious consequence. Underlying that conclusion are three assumptions about antidumping:

1. Antidumping regulations have a legitimate function. In this view the regulations are based on "fairness" and make "obvious" sense (see chapter 2). The idea that a product should have the same price in all markets appeals to many people. As a result, offsetting price differences by antidumping duties seems to them to be a restrained reaction. Indeed, that idea is so engrained that antidumping officials in the European Union, who sometimes impose antidumping duties lower than dumping margins, have a sense of their own generosity that survives demonstration that EU dumping margins themselves are grossly exaggerated.

2. Only a very small fraction of imports are subject to antidumping measures: less than 1 percent in the European Union and 0.5 percent in the United States (Weidemann 1990 [EU]; U.S. International Trade Commission [ITC] 1995 [U.S.]). The antidumping authorities of the European Union and the United States lose no opportunity to stress this "fact," which will be scrutinized in this chapter.

3. Antidumping procedures follow a legal process and provide the same robust legal protection to plaintiffs and

defendants as any other court. To give the initiative to domestic producers by granting them a right to lodge the initial complaint seems normal. Investigation of such complaints by the public authorities seems to guarantee neutrality and impartiality, especially in countries whose residents are able to persuade themselves that the state is "benevolent" and cares for the "public interest."

This belief in antidumping action is reinforced by the WTO (and was by the GATT before it), which authorizes national antidumping regulations. The basis for those regulations is first elaborated at the world level, within the GATT–WTO arena, and accepted by the European Union, Japan, the United States, and all other WTO members. In these circumstances, it is thought, antidumping legislation must be properly drawn up and legally sound; regulations so well founded cannot be bad.

Dr. Jekyll seemed a good and compassionate doctor. His monstrous nature emerged only slowly, so it took time before anyone realized that Mr. Hyde endangered the lives of his relatives and friends. Likewise, when these widely accepted beliefs about antidumping regulations are subjected to closer examination, the story that emerges is much less pleasant.

Proportion of Trade Affected by Antidumping

Large firms spend huge sums on antidumping (whether as plaintiffs or as defendants). In contrast, national antidumping measures apply only to small percentages of trade. How can this minute trade coverage be consistent with these expenditures? An obvious possibility is that the official figures do not give the right picture of trade coverage. Indeed, on examination, the official figures turn out to be highly suspect. They are subject to three computational biases.

First, the denominator is inflated. It includes trade in

goods that are not produced in the importing countries and therefore are not subject to antidumping. And it includes trade in agriculture, which is so heavily protected that there is no call for antidumping measures, at least in the European Union. (Several agricultural products are subject to U.S. antidumping measures, such as orange juice, apples, fish, wheat, beef, and cut flowers.) Second, the numerator is deflated. It is based on the level of imports *after* antidumping measures, which is likely to be considerably lower than the level before the measures. Antidumping measures are typically restrictive—the average antidumping duty is roughly 20–25 percent in the European Union and 30–35 percent in the United States, with many peaks higher than 50 percent in both countries. And third, the levels are averages with respect to all trade partners. Hence, they ignore the highly discriminatory factor of antidumping measures that cause some countries to be targeted much more frequently than others—for example, those in Asia and Central and Eastern Europe. Once these factors are taken into account, the trade coverage of antidumping actions is much larger.

In the European Union, for instance, oil and farm imports represent more than 20 percent of total imports from outside Europe, and, on average, imports of goods subject to antidumping measures were reduced by 30 percent over the three years following the imposition of antidumping measures. After simple adjustment of the official trade coverage to take account of these facts, the annual antidumping coverage amounts to almost 2 percent, which has to be cumulated over five years (since antidumping measures are generally enforced for a minimum of five years). This figure is still an average for all trading partners: the coverage of antidumping measures for particular trading partners or periods can be much higher, up to 25 percent for industrial exports of the former Soviet Union.

Antidumping actions are thus much more significant

than is officially stated. Even the better estimates just suggested, however, offer an unduly narrow view of the real effect of antidumping action. Modern protectionism, like modern military art, relies on a different technology from that of a few centuries ago. From the Middle Ages to the nineteenth century, high, then wide, walls were key to European military power, and uniformly high tariff walls were the key mercantilist tool. Now, military strength lies in rockets guided by laser beams and almost undetectable planes, as illustrated by the Desert Storm operation in the Persian Gulf War. Protectionist tools have also evolved. Antidumping offers the capacity to target a good (and not the goods immediately before or after in the tariff classification) and a foreign firm (and not the others, which may be allies or subsidiaries of foreign companies with which complaining firms may have common interests in other products, or even subsidiaries of the domestic complaining firms).

Another way of estimating the coverage of antidumping cases is to look only at the major industries involved in the antidumping cases. Heavy-user industries—those that have lodged more than 5 percent of total antidumping cases—are the same in the United States and the European Union. Four industries—chemicals, primary and fabricated metals, nonelectrical machinery, and electrical and electronic equipment—represent 76 percent and 72 percent of the total number of antidumping cases brought in the United States and the European Union, respectively, between 1979 and 1989. The shares of each of these heavy users is roughly the same in both regions.

The concentration of antidumping cases in particular industries suggests an alternative approach for estimating the coverage of antidumping enforcement. Antidumping actions "chill" trade. Foreign exporters have good reason to behave cautiously when they face a few large import-competing firms willing to invest in antidumping actions. All imports that compete with the products of the heavy-user industries are likely to be reduced by the tight net of antidumping cases that confront them. The share of such imports in total manufacturing imports therefore provides a good proxy for the minimum-trade coverage of antidumping enforcement. The four heavy-user industries represent 10.5 percent of extra-EU imports and roughly 13 percent of value added.

This chilling effect, it might be argued, exists in all protectionist situations. The design of antidumping, however, drastically changes the nature of the threat. Determined domestic firms able to deploy expensive legal skills have the right and the capacity to lodge cases that are difficult to stop without strong political will. Moreover, the rate of "success" of the procedure (cases in which measures are imposed as a percentage of total cases lodged) is high. In the European Union, almost three cases out of four end with antidumping measures. In the United States from 1980 and 1992, the U.S. Department of Commerce made a total of 339 final antidumping determinations, of which 315 (93 percent) were affirmative. Injury was found in 66 percent of the affirmative cases, so duties were imposed in 62 percent of the cases that reached a final determination (U.S. Congressional Budget Office 1994, 50).

The threat is amplified by the huge margins of dumping that the authorities claim to discover. Average dumping margins (excluding reviews) are 33 percent for the United States and 37 percent for the European Union.[1] Furthermore, they have increased over time: U.S. cases exhibit trade-weighted average dumping margins of 20.9 percent in 1980–1985, 32.8 percent in 1986–1990, and 37.7 percent in 1991–1993, and trade-weighted averages are systematically biased toward underestimation (ITC 1995).

---

1. The figure for the United States is based on the unweighted average of 105 antidumping cases examined by Morkre and Kelly (1994). On the EU situation, see Bourgeois and Messerlin (1994).

Indeed, levels of antidumping protection—when they are known—are two to three times the level of protection granted by the WTO most-favored-nation tariffs included in the tariff schedules of the countries imposing antidumping measures. The peaks, it seems, are stupendous: margins of dumping and duties can exceed 100 percent. These levels reflect a highly distorted tariff structure. In U.S. cases initiated during the years 1989–1993, the weighted average dumping margin was 162 percent on affected imports from India, and 106 percent on affected imports from the Netherlands (ITC 1995, 38 [table 3.3]).

In such circumstances, it is not astonishing that the chilling effect is considerable. In the United States, imported quantities declined by 73 percent and unit values increased by 32.7 percent for imports with high calculated dumping margins. For imports with medium calculated margins, the corresponding figures are 21 percent and 1.8 percent, and they are 3.2 percent and 2.9 percent for cases terminated without official measures. Interestingly, cases with alleged low margins show a decline in both quantity and price (16.4 percent and 9.7 percent, respectively) (ITC 1995, 38 [3.3]).

On the EU side, imported quantities fell by 36 percent on average in the third year after the initiation of antidumping, and prices increased by 12 percent in the fifth year (Messerlin 1989, 563–87). As in the United States, trade declined even when cases were terminated without official measures: by almost 10 percent after the first year and by 35 percent after the fifth year.

Not Stable Law, but Ever-changing Regulations

The notions on which antidumping actions are based may look sensible to casual observers. In fact, they make no sense at all, as is evident from past antidumping cases and reviews.

Cases and Reviews. To make matters worse, the actual process is far from a simple matter of opening a case against producers of a good in one country, deciding whether to apply antidumping measures, and enforcing such measures, if necessary. A case can be opened against producers in one country, and then a few months later be "extended" to other countries. As soon as a case is opened, therefore, *all* exporters of the product, regardless of country, wonder whether they will be caught in the net. Such fears are not limited to countries producing the good in question: "transit" countries, through which exports pass before being imported in the initiating country, may also become involved.

The European Union provides some remarkable examples of the complexity of this opening procedure. A case in point is one opened in 1988 against calcium metal imports from Russia and the People's Republic of China and terminated with the imposition of antidumping duties (roughly 22 percent). One EU importer (Extramet, a French firm) then went to the European Court of Justice and to the French Council for Competition, arguing that the complainant (Péchiney, a French nationalized firm) was refusing to sell calcium metal to Extramet and aimed to block imports in order to exert its dominant market power. In June 1992 the court ruled that Extramet was right and it repealed the antidumping duties. A logical interpretation of the court ruling is that the case was closed. The European Commission, however, took the ruling to mean that the investigation could be reopened, and in November 1992 it initiated a "new" case.

Because "reviews" are allowed, closing a case can be as opaque as opening a case. The European Union is particularly interesting in this regard: its regulations contain a "sunset" clause stipulating that a case is closed after five years, unless a review concludes that the antidumping measures should be renewed. In other words, the review process counterbalances the sunset clause. This exception can have substantial repercussions: between 1970 and 1989 the European Union permitted 152 reviews, as against 560 newly initiated cases, and 83 of these 152 reviews corresponded to only to 38 initial cases. Reviews can extend cases indefinitely (as can private agreements, though in an even less transparent way).

Have reviews been an instrument for harassing the exporters caught in the initial cases? In the European Union, reviews arise only after an antidumping complaint has been initiated and discharged (by imposition of a duty, acceptance of an undertaking, or without restrictive measures). They are initiated after the European Commission has received a request to do so by foreign or EU firms, EU users, member states, or the commission itself. Reviews are thus different from the "initial" cases: they require specific complaints from EU firms or foreign exporters, they must be based on new information, they require a commission ruling that the review is warranted, they do not necessarily involve all countries included in the initial case, and the review mechanism may be made more complex by including in the same review firms or countries involved in different initial cases.

That reviews can be initiated on the request of foreign firms seems on the face of it to be clearly favorable to foreign exporters. Initiations by foreign firms, however, represent only one-tenth of EU reviews during the period 1980–1989, and the vast majority of these reviews (three-quarters) have been terminated by restrictive measures. This poor success rate may explain why requests for reviews by foreign firms have declined.

A comparison of reviews initiated by EU firms or institutions (member states, or the commission) and the initial cases confirms this negative impression. First, reviews are even more highly concentrated by industry than initial cases (with a couple of industries—sawmills and pulp and paper—much more active than others, having requested roughly as many reviews as initial cases). Second, the measures complainants have obtained in the wake of reviews are more numerous (by a factor of 20 percent) and more restrictive than in the initial cases.

Particular reviews show just how far the procedure has been used as an instrument of harassment. A complaint initiated in 1978 about exports of a wood product (fiber building board) against eight countries generated twenty distinct reviews (in 1981, 1983, 1984, 1985, 1988, and 1989). The countries most frequently caught in these reviews were Sweden, Czechoslovakia, Finland, Poland, and the USSR—all countries likely to have a comparative advantage in wood products. In the 1989 review, the European Commission stated: "The changed circumstances [observed during a previous 1988 review] have led the Commission to consider that a review should also be carried out in respect of the rest of the countries for which antidumping measures concerning imports of hardboard into the Community are in force. This should be done in order *to ensure non-discrimination* with regard to these countries" (*EC Official Journal* 1989; emphasis added). This is a good illustration of the profound "GATT-inconsistency" of antidumping actions. Nondiscrimination is no longer related to the most favored nation, but to the most "unfavored" nation.

Links between Cases and Reviews. The traditional way of counting antidumping cases treats cases as though they are independent of one another. It conceals the tight links between cases and between cases and reviews, and it masks the distorting effect that antidumping measures can have on markets in closely related products. These distortions may in turn generate additional forces for dumping (price discrimination) in these related goods, and thus for more antidumping cases.

These various domino effects in antidumping enforcement are well illustrated by the 1989 EU review on ball bearings originating in Singapore. The notice of initiation in that case explicitly mentions two reasons for the review. First, the "imposition of a high antidumping duty by the Department of Commerce on exports to the United States (25.08 percent) will lead to a significant part of this production being switched to exports towards the Community." Second, it cites the risk that exports from Singapore to the European Union "may increase if the current EU proceedings against Thailand were to lead to the imposition of antidumping or anti-subsidy duties" (*EC Official Journal* 1990). It would hardly be possible to be more explicit.

Catching all the links requires a deep knowledge of the technology involved, including the technology em-bodied in firm plants. In the absence of such a knowledge, two proxies can be provided.

- First, there are two easily identifiable (though in-complete) sources of links. New cases can expand the geographic scope of old cases. The 1988 EU hexameth-ylene tetramine case, for instance, reinitiated a 1982 case on the same product that had expired in 1988 and ex-panded the country list to Bulgaria, Hungary, Poland, and Yugoslavia (though it eliminated East Germany and the USSR). New cases can also expand product coverage. A sequence of cases lodged by three EU firms in the tung-sten industry in 1988 illustrates this—seven cases in a row concerning six closely related products (ammonium para-tungstate, tungstic oxide and acid, tungsten metal powder, and tungsten carbide and fused tungsten carbide).

- Second, links between cases can be revealed by ele-mentary technological links. As an example, table 3–1 pre-sents a short list of the main chemical products subject to EU antidumping actions. This industry is riddled with antidumping cases and reviews.

Nontransparent Measures. Restrictive antidumping out-comes consist of duties, undertakings, and other mea-

TABLE 3–1

"LINEAGE" IN EC ANTIDUMPING CASES IN THE CHEMICAL INDUSTRY,
1970–1989

Products	Years of Antidumping Cases
Dry gas products	
Fuel gas	
Methanol	
MTBE	
Formaldehyde	1984
Melamine	
Phenol formaldehyde	
Polyacetal resins	
Urea formaldehyde	
Alkyd resins	
Pentaerythritol	1983
Tertio amyl methyl ether	
Ammonia	
Urea	1986
Urea formaldehyde	
Fertilizer	1980
Melamine	
Hexamethylene diamine	
Nylon 66	
Nitric acid	1989
Nitrobenzen	
Nitroparafin	
Ammonium nitrate	
Acrylonitrile	1982
Acrylic resins	1985
Nitrile resins	
ABS resins	
Hexamethylene tetramine	1982, 1988
Explosives	
Phenolic resins	
Pharmaceutical	
Aromatic products	
Benzene	
Other chemicals	
Caprolectum	

(*table continues*)

TABLE 3–1 (continued)

Products	Years of Antidumping Cases
Styrene	1980
Phenol	1981
Maleic anhydride	
Toluene	
Paraxylene	1980
DMT	
Terephtalic acid	
Polyester	
Orthoxylene	1980
Phtalic anhydride	
M-xylene	
Isophtalic anhydride	
Fractionary products	
Ethane	
Ethylene	1981, 1982
Low density polyethylene	1982
High density polyethylene	1982
Ethylene oxide	
Ethylene glycol	1980, 1986, 1987
Polyester resins	1987, 1988
Ethylene dichloride	
Vinyl chloride monomer	
Polyvinyl chloride	1981
Ethyl benzene	
Styrene	1980
Polystyrene	1984
Styrene butadiene rubber	
Ethanol	
Linear alpha olefins	
Detergents	
Ethylene chloride	
Acetaldehyde	
Acetic anhydrid	
Pentaerythritol	1983
Vinyl acetate monomer	1980, 1983
Polyvinyl acetate	
Butene	

TABLE 3–1 (continued)

Products	Years of Antidumping Cases
Butane	
Isobutylene	
MTDE	
Di isobutylene	
Tri isobutylene	
Polymers	
Butadiene	
Styrene butadiene rubber	
Polybutadiene rubber	
Hexamethylene diamine	
Nylon salt	
Chloroprine	
Propylene	
Polypropylene	1981
Acrylonitrile	1982
Acrylic acid	
Propylene oxide	
Butaldehyde	
Di ethyl hexanol	
Cumene	
Phenol	1981
Caprolectum	
Acetone	
Methacrylate	
Isopropanol	
Alkyl chloride	

SOURCE: *EC Official Journal,* various issues.

sures. Duties can be ad valorem (expressed as a percentage of prices) or specific (a particular monetary amount). Ad valorem duties are transparent: they give easily available information on the differences between world prices and those within the European Union. Specific duties are less transparent: they give information on the amount of duty, but information on import prices is needed before the percentage value of the wedge between world and domestic prices can be computed.

Undertakings are opaque. The actual content of undertakings is never published. Official decisions may indicate the form of an undertaking—whether it places a floor on prices or a ceiling on imports—but do not necessarily do so. When they do provide that information, it is often in terms so obscure that no one not directly involved in the cases can be confident of correctly interpreting them. Hence only firms involved in the cases can estimate the ad valorem equivalents of undertakings with confidence, and they are generally not eager to reveal that information, either because they are domestic firms enjoying protection, because they are foreign firms benefiting from the rents associated with this kind of instrument, or because they fear some retaliation from import-competing firms if they divulge the content of the undertakings.

The lack of transparency of undertakings is accentuated by the fact that undertakings are difficult to monitor, particularly when they take the form of price agreements that can be bypassed by the confidentiality of private contracts. As a result, the ad valorem equivalents of undertakings are likely to vary over time, inasmuch as undertakings by foreign exporters—though always said to be voluntary—presumably vary in their degree of "voluntariness."

Between 1980 and 1987, undertakings accounted for more than half of all the outcomes of EU antidumping cases and almost 75 percent of all restrictive outcomes. Since 1987, the increasing use of duties suggests progress toward GATT transparency. The question arising in the wake of this progress is whether the *form* of protection has been accompanied by a change in the *level* of protection during the period 1987–1989.

A crude estimate of the voluntariness of undertakings is provided by two proxies. Imposing provisional duties before undertakings is likely to give the European Commission leverage on the concerned firms. Imposing measures on some exporters is likely to exert a deterrent effect on the rest of the firms, even if they are not directly involved in the same cases. The penalty imposed by the European Union can thus reasonably be considered at its highest when undertakings are preceded by provisional duties. Less restrictive is the combination of undertakings and definitive duties, since definitive duties in these cases are a way by which the European Commission and European Council may support the pure price-quantity private maintenance schemes between the other firms involved. The least restrictive of these penalties is undertakings alone, which are pure price-quantity private maintenance schemes. Indeed, the period from 1980 to 1986 witnessed an erosion of the undertakings alone and a quasi disappearance of the undertakings mixed with definitive duties, which are in sharp contrast to a surge in undertakings preceded by provisional duties (corresponding to the highest penalty).

Discrimination. The "spaceship" nature of antidumping actions—they are highly discriminatory and tend to be specific to trading partners and firms—has profound implications for the world trade system. They undermine both of the two WTO basic rules, the principles of bound tariffs and nondiscrimination. The power of antidumping enforcement to discriminate is endless. In the European Union, antidumping cases initiated between 1980 and 1988 involved almost 1,100 items at the six-digit level of the EU tariff classification (NIMEXE, at this time), which included roughly 7,000 items. On average, each case involved two countries, so these antidumping measures were equivalent to the creation of 2,200 new tariff lines. Even that is a gross underestimate: different antidumping measures can be imposed on different firms, and indeed they generally are. On average, each case involves three to four reported foreign firms. In other words, antidumping measures have generated between 3,300 and 4,000 extra-tariff lines, or almost half of the existing tariff classification. Also note that *all* the *relative* levels of protection have changed: imports on which no measures were taken have

41

been relatively deprotected in relation to goods protected by antidumping measures.

"Privatization" of Antidumping

Antidumping "laws" defending the "public interest" are a myth. Antidumping action has been captured by firms. Protection has always been private in the sense that it is granted to private interests despite welfare losses imposed on the importing country as a whole. Antidumping regulations do more, however. By design, they enable import-competing firms to choose the "right" target at the right time in the right case for defending their interests. As a result, import-competing firms tend to consider anti-dumping actions an integral part of their corporate strategies (to the point that managers who lodge antidumping complaints are seen as successful operators).

From this point of view, evidence from the EU experience is particularly valuable because the Uruguay Round antidumping agreement has introduced provisions indicating who can lodge a complaint that are close to the internal guidelines followed by the EU antidumping authorities over the past two decades. Since 1980 most anti-dumping decisions published in the EU's *Official Journal* mention the name of the major complaining firms. This information provides a clear picture of the "who's who" in antidumping enforcement. Parent companies are directly involved in some antidumping cases, whereas subsidiaries take the lead in other cases. Clearly, it is more appropriate for the parent companies to do so, because decisions to lodge an antidumping complaint are likely to be taken at the highest levels. There are many reasons for that: complaints are costly, they require the presentation of industrial and financial information that can be confidential, they are likely to have long-term consequences on industrial relationships between parent companies, and several subsidiaries of the same parent company may be involved in the same case. This last observation suggests that parent companies are the ones in charge. (There are even cases in which the subsidiaries of one firm in the various member states are the only complaining firms!) Table 3–2 identifies the major complaining parent companies in the four industries that are heavy users of EU antidumping cases. It suggests four interesting points.

First, antidumping enforcement is a matter of corporate strategy: a few large firms are behind a high proportion of complaints. Hoechst, for instance, is a complainant in 87 percent of the cases in the synthetic chemical industry, Philips and Thomson in 70 percent of the cases in radios and TVs, Arbed in 39 percent of the steel cases, and Montedison in 23 percent of those in industrial chemicals.

Second, among these few firms, even fewer have voiced complaints over the entire period considered (the others have been complainants for only a couple of years). The steel and radio and TV industries appear to be dominated by "frequent" complainants, and the two chemical industries have a "hard core" of six frequent complainants: Bayer, ENI, Hoechst, ICI, Montedison, and Rhone-Poulenc. The other firms have been active more episodically, most notably during the crisis of 1981–1983. Though it is not possible to provide comparable figures for the United States (in particular, because of the more prominent role of ad hoc committees), it is nevertheless clear that there is the same phenomenon: Armco, Atlantic Steel, Bethlehem, Georgetown, LTV, and U.S. Steel are dominating the steel cases, and Du Pont or Hercules the chemical cases.

Third, the capture of antidumping enforcement by these few complaining firms would be understated if their capacity to oppose antidumping actions on their inputs were ignored. The 1982 acrylonitrile case is one of the few in which the end user's interests have been taken into account; no antidumping measure was imposed here.

Fourth, surprisingly few of the large non-EU firms

TABLE 3-2
"WHO'S WHO" OF COMPLAINING FIRMS IN EC ANTIDUMPING CASES,
1980–1989

Parent Companies	Origin Countries	Frequency (%)
Industrial chemicals (93 cases)		
Montedison	Italy	23.7
ENI	Italy	21.5
Péchiney	France	19.4
Rhône-Poulenc	France	17.2
Alusuisse	Switzerland	15.1
Brit. Petroleum	Britain	15.1
Hoechst	Germany	12.9
ICI	Britain	12.9
Steel (41 cases)		
Arbed	Luxemburg	39.0
Thyssen	Germany	36.6
Salzgitter	Germany	22.0
Italsider	Italy	14.6
Hoogovens	Netherlands	12.2
Usinor	France	12.2
Synthetic fibers (31 cases)		
Hoechst	Germany	87.0
Montedison	Italy	71.0
Rhône-Poulenc	France	51.6
Du Pont	U.S.A.	48.4
ENI	Italy	45.2
Akzo	Netherlands	32.3
Bayer	Germany	29.0
ICI	Britain	29.0
Consumer electronics (10 cases)		
Philips	Netherlands	70.0
Thomson	France	70.0
Nokia	Finland	50.0
AEG	Germany	20.0
Motorola	U.S.A.	10.0
Siemens	Germany	10.0

SOURCES: *EC Official Journal,* various issues, "Who Owns Whom," and authors' calculations.

have been major users of the EU antidumping laws, either directly or through subsidiaries: Alusuisse, Du Pont, Esso, Norsk Hydro, Nokia, and Motorola. The same phenomenon can be observed in the United States, even to a greater extent: most of the complaints in the chemical industries are lodged by EU firms, such as BASF, Hoechst, ICI, Monsanto, and Rhône-Poulenc—sometimes exclusively against EU exports. In what circumstances, then, is a non-EU firm considered European enough to be authorized to lodge a complaint? Can it do so alone or must it be with other firms? What factors prompt a joint complaint?

In one complaint involving copier firms, Xerox was considered an EU firm whereas Canon was not. Yet at the time both had their parent companies outside the European Union (Xerox in the United States and Canon in Japan); both were the leading EU producers (two plants each, with a total production of 80,000 and 70,000 units for Xerox and Canon, respectively, or roughly 80 percent of total EU production); and both were importing a large quantity of copiers from their subsidiaries in Japan (Fuji-Xerox for Xerox and Canon-Japan for Canon)—with Xerox-EU importing Japanese parts.

Antidumping as a corporate strategy smacks of an effort by complaining firms to capture not only trade policy but also industrial policy. A striking feature of this capture is that it is likely to lead to the most suicidal type of industrial policy, because the discriminatory nature of antidumping measures implies that antidumping is destructive of some of the domestic interests.

This point is well illustrated by the U.S. flat panel display (FPD) case. In 1990, seven U.S. FPD producers lodged an antidumping complaint against thirteen Japanese competitors for dumping; and at first glance it may seem plausible that predatory dumping occurred. All the U.S. plaintiffs were tiny firms; by contrast, the Japanese defendants included giants, such as Toshiba, Sanyo, and

Hitachi, and altogether they represented 90 percent of the liquid crystal FPD world output. But a more careful look at the facts annihilates this first impression. The small number of U.S. complainants and their small size were the consequence of a conscious business strategy followed by all the other U.S. firms previously involved in FPD production. From 1980 to 1989, the fifteen largest U.S. computer producers decided to close or sell their FPD plants for three reasons: FPDs were not central to their business strategy; their production would not be profitable because of fierce competition; and it would be easy to buy FPDs at reasonable prices and delays. Of course, the last point mirrors the argument about fierce competition, which deserves more attention. If, globally, the Japanese producers represented 90 percent of liquid crystal FPD world output, their individual market shares ranged from 1 to 15 percent. That suggests a strongly competitive market (Hart 1993): indeed, in 1990, the Herfindahl index based on the Japanese market shares of liquid crystal FPDs can be estimated at 0.12, far below the threshold (0.18) triggering investigation for possible anticompetitive behavior in the U.S. antitrust law.

As often in antidumping investigations, however, these basic facts were misinterpreted. Despite much discussion of the degree of substitutability between FPDs produced by U.S. and Japanese firms, little weight was given to that factor in the final decision, as noted by U.S. International Trade Commission Acting Chairman Anne Brunsdale in her dissenting views (ITC 1991, 29–33). Price competition between Japanese firms was seen as proving the existence of dumping, whereas it reflected the intensity of the struggles for survival in this market. The rise of imports from Japan was perceived as a proof of injury, not as a logical consequence of the specialization policy chosen by the large U.S. firms. Lastly, the notion of predation was stretched to its limits: U.S. complaining firms argued that the mere existence of Japanese firms was depriving them of any chance to get the huge amount of capital they would need for producing large amounts of FPDs. That recalls the old story of candlemakers lodging a petition against the unfair competition of the sun (Bastiat 1854). Of course, the U.S. complainants would have been better off without the existence of Japanese FPD producers, as would the candlemakers in the absence of the sun. But that is not the point. As bluntly stated by the Apple representative in the U.S. ITC hearings, OIS (one of the small U.S. complainants) had "zero high volume manufacturing capability, little customer support experience, zero manufacturing flexibility, zero mass production experience and delivery schedule" (ITC 1991, 36). No private bank would be eager to give loans to such a firm.

High antidumping duties (62.7 percent) were imposed on the largest subset of FPDs—the active matrix LCDs (AM-LCD), which were produced by only *two* of these seven small U.S. producers. Lower duties (7 percent) were imposed on electroluminescent FPDs, the other subset of FPDs (for which the Japanese firms represented only 30 percent of world output). In sum, two small U.S. firms were able to impose very high costs on the U.S. AM-LCD users, which happen to be all the major U.S. producers of laptops. To avoid these costs, several of these large U.S. firms, such as Apple, IBM, and Compaq, upgraded their laptop facilities offshore (assembled laptops were not subject to antidumping duties). In other words, other countries (ironically, Japan was one of them) were the main beneficiaries of the U.S. antidumping measures.

The story does not stop there. First, in 1993, a large glass firm bought OIS, putting an end to the antidumping duties on the AM-LCD FPDs, and revealing the waste of resources associated with this case. Second, in 1994, the antidumping case got an heir, under the form of a classic industrial policy scenario: in April, the U.S. administration unveiled a $587 million initiative to create an FPD industry in the United States by the year 2000 (Flamm

1994). The initial reason invoked was "national security" and the need of a secure supply of FPDs for the Department of Defense (DOD). As the DOD demand represented only 5 percent of the total FPD market, however, it was argued that creating such a small captive supply capability for military needs would mean high unit costs forever. As a result, it was suggested that the national security goal should be stretched to the objective of a "technology policy," with a targeted market share for the U.S. FPD industry of 15 percent of the world FPD market by the year 2000. Barfield (1994) has shown the many flaws of such a policy: its ignorance of weighing FPD priorities against other DOD priorities; its uncertainty (to say the least) about picking winners; its inability to second-guess the markets (there are many markets for such a differentiable product, with very different parameters in terms of technical features, prices, and marketing; and its consequences in terms of violation of WTO rules and domestic traditions in terms of subsidies (using the various figures suggested, the rate of subsidization would range from 7 percent, if everything had gone according to plan, to 30 percent at least, if things had turned bad). General cuts in the U.S. budget aborted this industrial policy scheme.

This almost perfect illustration of antidumping as industrial policy deserves a last remark. There is a deep irony in the fact that the arguments used by the proponents of the industrial policy were consistent with the arguments of the *defendants* (*not* of the complainants) in the antidumping case. In other words, the arguments advanced by the proponents of industrial policy pledged *against* antidumping measures. First, the industrial policy debate recognizes that DOD needs "customized" products (produced by U.S. plaintiffs): that implies that imported and domestic FPDs were not like-products, as underlined by the Japanese defendants. Second, the industrial policy proponents stress the point that "very minor changes in technology, manufacturing, and market parameters can cause huge swings in the rate of return": that strongly suggests that computing margins on the basis of constructed costs was a fallacy, and that predation was an incorrect analysis of the functioning of the FPD market. Lastly, public subsidies were said to be necessary because the "rate of return on investment is extremely uncertain for potential producers with no previous experience." That seems a strong *ex post* support of the position of the U.S. defendants arguing that the small U.S. producers were unlikely to get the capital they wanted—hence, that there was no predation, except that of unreasonable dreams (Flamm 1994).

The auto-destructive capacity of antidumping cases does not need an elaborated industrial policy, as in the FPD case. It can follow from the mere sequence of events and cases, as best illustrated by the EC calcium metal case mentioned earlier.

Existing EU antidumping duties protect Péchiney from its EU competitor Extramet by raising the cost of Chinese and Russian calcium metal. But there are two other world producers of calcium products—in Canada and in the United States. These two producers could sell their calcium metal in the European Union. Although this calcium metal is expensive compared with the Chinese and Russian products, it is still less expensive than the EU calcium metal produced by Péchiney behind antidumping duties. In addition, the North American firms could use the cheap calcium metal they buy from China and Russia in order to produce and sell finished calcium products in the EU market at a lower price than similar calcium metal from Péchiney. In sum, the EU antidumping case has helped Péchiney eliminate its more efficient EU competitor Extramet from the EU market, but it will also help the North American firms eliminate Péchiney from the EU market. It is hard to see the benefit of such an industrial policy for EU firms and governments, more especially as Péchiney could react by launching a new antidumping

TABLE 3–3

Number of Antidumping Cases Initiated and Terminated by Measures, the United States and the European Community, 1979–1989

Industries	United States				European Community			
	Cases initiated		Cases terminated by measures[a]		Cases initiated		Cases terminated by measures[a]	
	Number	Share[b]	Number	Rate of success[c]	Number	Share[b]	Number	Rate of success[c]
Chemical	69	15.3	40	58.0	155	40.3	121	78.1
Metal	224	49.7	162	72.3	57	14.8	37	64.9
Nonelectrical machinery	27	6.0	21	77.8	34	8.8	24	70.6
Electrical equipment	24	5.3	17	70.8	33	8.6	24	72.7
The four industries	344	76.3	240	69.8	279	72.5	206	73.8
All industries	451	100.0	275	61.0	385	100.0	270	70.1

a. Including cases terminated by the complainants' withdrawal.

b. As a percentage of the total number of cases initiated.

c. Cases terminated by measures as a percentage of the total number of cases.

SOURCES: H. J. Shin, "Antidumping Law and Foreign Behaviour: An Empirical Analysis'' (Ph.D. diss., Yale University, 1994); Jacques Bourgeois and Patrick A. Messerlin, "Competition and the EC Antidumping Regulations'' Collège Européen de Bruges and Institut d'Etudes Politiques de Paris, 1993, mimeo; and authors' calculations.

case against North American producers, in an endless *fuite en avant* (headlong rush)—as Hyde finally overthrows Jekyll.[2]

Mr. Hyde Has Overthrown Dr. Jekyll

In sum, antidumping regulations show a strong protectionist drift, in that antidumping cases are concentrated in a few industries, and restrictive measures are almost sure to be adopted at the end of the procedures. As table 3–3 shows, a handful of industries lodge 70 percent of the cases initiated in the European Union or the United States. Trade restrictive measures as the result of these antidumping actions are even more concentrated than the cases brought. In the European Union, restrictive outcomes are 11.9 percent more frequent in the core set of industries lodging many antidumping cases.

This global result deserves one final comment. Cases and restrictive measures against a given country tend to be less frequent as time goes on. This pattern would not suggest that there are "recidivist" dumpers (countries more willing to dump repeatedly than others), a crucial issue in the Uruguay Round negotiations. It does suggest that an increasing proportion of the complaints were not justified. In other words, it is not the dumpers who are recidivist, but the antidumpers.

---

2. To complete the discussion, Péchiney faces another possibility: the North American firms may decide not to penetrate the EU market, in generating a world collusion or even cartel. Péchiney would then be in the weak position of the marginal firm.

4

Antidumping in the Uruguay Round

Traditional advocacy of antidumping is based on the idea that antidumping defends weak domestic interests against powerful foreign ones. The reality is different. The reality is that antidumping is a weapon used by powerful domestic interests to stifle foreign competition.

The core problem in this context is that antidumping authorities have the ability to bias their calculations to find dumping and injury where there has been no dumping and no injury. They are therefore able to apply trade-reducing "remedies" almost at will.

This state of affairs does not only affect products that are targets of formal antidumping proceedings. Exporters whose products are subject to antidumping must face high costs—the legal costs of defense as well as the commercial costs of restrictions on competitive ability.[1] Exporters of products that have not yet been targets of formal antidumping proceedings will try to reduce the probability of their becoming targets, and to increase the probability that if they do become targets, they will be found not to be dumped or not to have injured the domestic industry. They will therefore charge higher prices

---

1. A practicing U.S. antidumping lawyer comments: "An exporter wishing to respond adequately to a lengthy U.S. antidumping questionnaire will need the services of lawyers, an accountant, an economist and a computer programmer, in addition to its own personnel. It will need to work night and day, seven days a week, for extended periods" (Palmeter 1995, 71).

than they would in the absence of antidumping, and will pull their competitive punches in other ways.

This concealed protectionist effect of antidumping, moreover, is multiplied by the interaction of antidumping with other instruments of contingent protection.

Safeguards and Voluntary Export Restraints

The GATT contains a number of safeguard clauses, setting out conditions in which a WTO member may temporarily withdraw from its obligations. In the context of antidumping, Article XIX is the most important of these. It authorizes WTO members to increase their protection against ". . . any product that is imported into the territory of that contracting party in such increased quantities and under such conditions as to cause or threaten serious injury to domestic producers. . . ."

Article XIX. Despite the GATT-consistent means of coping with troublesome imports that it offers, Article XIX was little used before the Uruguay Round. Two reasons are generally considered to account for that neglect.

First, as formulated before the Uruguay Round, Article XIX required similar treatment of similar imports from different sources: a government invoking Article XIX could not treat widgets from country *A* differently from imports of widgets from country *B*. A government with a political problem connected with imports, however, will often value good relations with some exporting countries more highly than with others, and would like to treat them differently. Governments often see problems with imports as stemming from an increase in the exports of one "disruptive" country, moreover, and want to act against imports from that country only.

Second, countries whose exports were affected by an Article XIX action could claim "compensation." An exporting country could claim a reduction in the duty im-

posed on another of its exports by the country invoking
Article XIX, or it could increase its duty on a good exported to it by that country. Either route reduced the political attraction of Article XIX actions. Like other people,
politicians prefer to give gifts without a bill attached.
Being seen to give with one hand and take away with the
other has a more limited appeal.

Voluntary Export Restraints. Before the Uruguay Round,
the governments of developed countries used "voluntary
export restraints" (VERs) much more frequently than Article XIX. When they might have invoked Article XIX to
restrict imports at their own borders, they preferred to
ask the exporting-country government (or sometimes the
exporting industry itself) to restrict the volume of exports.

VERs were not authorized by the GATT, and the widespread use of an instrument that was not GATT-consistent
(VERs), rather than one that was (Article XIX), was an
embarrassment for the GATT. From the standpoint of national politicians, though, the advantages of VERs are easy
to see. A request to restrict exports could be extended to
one or to all exporting countries: no legal rule prevented
an importing-country government from discriminating
between them. Nor did it have to compensate exporting
countries by such politically unattractive means as reduc-
tions in its tariff on other goods, or increases in foreign
tariffs on its exports.

Why, though, would the government of an exporting
country ever agree to restrict its exports? How might it be
in its interest, or in the interest of the exporting industry,
to do so?

One set of reasons is economic. A VER typically allows
the price of the restricted export to rise in the importing-
country market, and in a variety of circumstances, the
profits of the exporting industry will also rise. Second, and
in the present context more relevant, a VER might be

worse than the *status quo*, viewed from the standpoint of the exporting-country government and industry, but might nevertheless be superior to the alternative methods of restriction that the GATT made legally available to the importing country.

These "alternative methods of restriction," however, included antidumping. An importing-country government could threaten antidumping if a VER were refused. Faced with such a threat, exporting-country governments and exporting industries often preferred to accept a VER rather than subject the exporting industry to the rigors of antidumping.

If threats of antidumping action are credible and effective, moreover, no formal VER is needed to achieve the reduction in exports desired by the importing-country government. If national or multilateral controls on use of antidumping are loose, an importing-country government need do no more than inform an exporting-country government—or the exporting industry—that it will initiate antidumping unless exports are restricted to a specified level. If that lower level is not substantially lower than the exporting-country government and the exporting industry believe would be the outcome of antidumping, they are likely to comply with the "request." Loose GATT or WTO controls on antidumping allow antidumping to be used as a policy substitute for VERs or Article XIX actions.

Contingent Protection in the Uruguay Round

The connections between neglect of Article XIX, expansion of VERs, and abuse of antidumping were central to the Uruguay Round. Widespread use of VERs and abuse of antidumping to obtain VERs or VER-like outcomes led to a potentially mortal loss of GATT credibility. This threat to the continued existence of the GATT contributed to one of the more dramatic outcomes of the Round—a ban on VERs.

Ban on VERs. Paragraph 22(b) of the *Agreement on Safeguards* says that

> A Member shall not seek, take or maintain any voluntary export restraints, orderly marketing agreements or any other similar measures on the export or the import side. These include actions taken by a single contracting party as well as actions under agreements, arrangements and understandings entered into by two or more Members.[2]

A footnote expands upon "similar measures," citing as examples ". . . export moderation, export-price or import-price monitoring systems, export or import surveillance, compulsory import cartels and discretionary export or import licensing schemes, any of which afford protection." Measures not conforming with the revised Article XIX must be phased out or brought into conformity within four years of the entry into force of the agreement.[3]

This seems to allow little compromise. The most notable remaining problem is that the WTO has no authority regarding nongovernmental agreements. Private agreements between national industries, without apparent involvement of governments, are therefore not affected by the ban.[4] Nevertheless, the ban places a heavy restric-

---

2. The Agreement is cited here as signed at Marrakech. In more recently printed versions, "paragraph 22" is the twenty-second paragraph of the Agreement, but is not referred to as such.

3. Each member may, however, maintain one nonconforming measure until December 31, 1999. The only such exception so far registered is an agreement between the EU and Japan regarding motor vehicles from Japan.

4. Paragraph 24 attempts to deal with this problem by calling on contracting parties "not [to] encourage nor support the adoption or maintenance by public or private enterprises of non-governmental measures equivalent to those referred to above." And Paragraph 32 says that "Any Member may notify the Committee on Safeguards of any non-governmental measures referred to in paragraph 24 above."

tion on VERs as such. A sensible working assumption, at this stage, is that VERs as such will cease to be a central feature of the global trading system.

Antidumping, though, can produce VER-like outcomes without the need for a formal VER. Moreover, under the Uruguay Round *Agreement on Interpretation of Article VI*, undertakings (suspension agreements in U.S. terminology) that have VER-like characteristics are perfectly legal. Article 8.1 says:

> Proceedings may be suspended or terminated without the imposition of provisional measures or antidumping duties upon receipt of satisfactory voluntary undertakings from an exporter to revise its prices or to cease exports to the area in question so that the authorities are satisfied that the injurious effect of the dumping is eliminated.

Getting rid of VERs does not get rid of protectionist pressures. The relevant question is how these pressures will be expressed if VERs cannot be used. If the ban on VERs is effective, governments must use Article XIX or antidumping to solve political problems caused by awkward imports. The choice they make is crucial for the future of the global trading system. Before likely choices can be assessed, however, the agreements reached in the Uruguay Round concerning Article XIX and antidumping must be examined.

Reform of Article XIX. The *Agreement on Safeguards* weakens Article XIX in some respects, in comparison with the pre-Uruguay Round formulation, but it toughens it in others.

Weakening Article XIX. The agreement weakens Article XIX by:

- Redefining the *conditions of application*: "A Member may apply a safeguard measure to a product only if that

Member has determined . . . that such a product is being imported into its territory in such increased quantities, *absolute or relative to domestic production*, and under such conditions as to cause or threaten to cause serious injury to the domestic industry that produces like or directly competitive products" (Paragraph 2: emphasis added). The emphasized words are an addition to the pre-Uruguay Round formulation, and they clearly weaken it.

• Restricting the right of affected exporters to *compensation*. Paragraph 18 says that the right to compensation ". . . shall not be exercised for the first three years that a safeguard measure is in effect, provided that the safeguard measure has been taken as a result of an absolute increase in imports. . . ." There was no restriction on the right to compensation before the Uruguay Round.

• Allowing *selectivity* (that is, discrimination between exporters). Under paragraph 9(a), an importing country applying a quota under Article XIX may seek agreement among exporters as to their share of a quota. In the likely event that "this method is not reasonably practicable," it allows the importer to allot shares in the quota on the basis of import shares "during a previous representative period . . . *due account being taken of any special factors which may have affected or may be affecting trade in the product*" (emphasis added). Moreover, paragraph 9(b) allows importing parties to ". . . depart from the provisions in 9(a) above provided that consultations . . . are conducted under the auspices of the Committee on Safeguards and that clear demonstration is provided to the Committee that

    (i)   imports from certain contracting parties have increased in disproportionate percentage in relation to the total increase of imports of the product concerned in the representative period,

    (ii) the reasons for the departure . . . are justified, and

    (iii) the conditions of such departure are equitable to all suppliers of the product concerned.

These provisions have no parallel in the pre-Uruguay Round GATT, and their effect is unclear. The nature of the "special factors which may have affected or may be affecting trade in the product" is not specified. Neither are the terms in which a departure from the general rule may be "justified," nor the criteria of equity under which a departure from the rule in paragraph 9(a) might be "equitable to all suppliers."

Strengthening Article XIX. In several other ways, however, Article XIX becomes tougher:

• The level of *transparency* is substantially increased. Article XIX may be used only after public hearings to determine whether the proposed measure is in the public interest. "The competent authorities shall publish a report setting forth their findings and reasoned conclusions reached on all pertinent issues of fact and law" (paragraph 3(a)). This is a completely new condition.

• The report must cover the issue of *injury*: "no determination of injury will be made . . . unless this investigation demonstrates, on the basis of objective evidence, the existence of the causal link between increased imports of the product concerned and serious injury or threat thereof." Again, the condition is completely new.

• Limits are placed on the *duration* of an Article XIX action. An Article XIX action must be terminated within eight years of its first application (paragraphs 10–12). When a product has already been protected under Article XIX, no new measures can be applied for a period equal to that during which the product was previously protected, or two years, whichever is longer (paragraph 14). Paragraph 21 requires the termination ". . . of all safeguard measures taken pursuant to Article XIX of the GATT 1947 not later than eight years after the date on which they were first applied or five years after the date of entry into force of the Agreement establishing the WTO, whichever comes later."

- There must be *progressive liberalization*: "In order to facilitate adjustment, if the expected duration of a safeguard measure . . . is over one year, it shall be progressively liberalized at regular intervals during the period of application" (paragraph 13). There was no parallel provision before the Uruguay Round.

- The appropriate level of *initial restrictions* is specified: "Safeguard measures shall be applied only to the extent as may be necessary [sic] to prevent or remedy serious injury and to facilitate adjustment. If a quantitative restriction is used, such a measure shall not reduce the quantity of imports below . . . the average of imports in the last three representative years for which statistics are available, unless clear justification is given that a different level is necessary to prevent or remedy serious injury" (Paragraph 8).

Reforms that toughen the conditions of application of Article XIX, however, also make it less attractive to governments with domestic problems created by imports. The alternative is antidumping; but if importing-country governments decide to use antidumping rather than Article XIX, the Uruguay-Round strategy will have failed. Success in forcing use of Article XIX depends on tightening access to antidumping.

Agreement on Antidumping

Controlling access to antidumping, however, is not easy.[5] To arrive at precisely defined rules through negotiation is

---

5. The discussion here refers only to the WTO *Agreement on Interpretation of Article VI*. National implementation of the agreement gives rise to further issues. Implementation in the United States is discussed by Palmeter (1995) and in the EU by Vermulst and Waer (1995) and Bronckers (1995). Horlick and Shea (1995) provide an authoritative discussion of the negotiation itself and commentary on some of the provisions that emerged from it.

difficult. Experience suggests, moreover, that in this area, national authorities will condition their actions on the strict letter of the law, not on its spirit; and that the loopholes that are an inevitable consequence of less-than-total precision will be fully exploited by them. The *Agreement on Interpretation of Article VI*, moreover, increases the importance of the letter of antidumping law by limiting the ability of dispute-settlement panels to examine the merits of a dispute concerning antidumping action. Article 17.6 says that when a panel examines an antidumping complaint:

(i)   in its assessment of the facts of the matter, the panel shall determine whether the authorities' assessment of the facts was proper and whether their evaluation of those facts was unbiased and objective. If the establishment of the facts was proper and the evaluation was unbiased and objective, even though the panel might have reached a different conclusion, the evaluation shall not be overturned;

(ii) the panel shall interpret the relevant provisions of the Agreement in accordance with the customary rules of interpretation of public international law. Where the panel finds that a relevant provision of the Agreement admits of more than one permissible interpretation, the panel shall find the authorities' measure to be in conformity with the Agreement if it rests upon one of these permissible interpretations.

Article 17.6 appears to give to national antidumping authorities all the leeway that the letter of the agreement allows.

The letter of laws and technical detail is crucial to antidumping practice. National antidumping regulations and the actions of national antidumping authorities over the next decade will probably reveal interpretations of the agreement that will allow it to be used for protectionist purposes, but that are now hidden in its words. Its actual force, therefore, will not be known for some years. The validity of a number of antidumping practices, however, was questioned before the Uruguay Round. Examination of the effect of the agreement on these practices offers a good first test of its strength.

Averaging. Products are not typically sold at a single price. Prices vary with market conditions at the time of the sale and other characteristics of the sale. To calculate a dumping margin, however, an antidumping authority must subtract "the" price in the export market from "the" price in the home market of the exporter. A natural solution is to take an average. The averages taken by antidumping authorities, however, are not straightforward.

One past practice, rationalized on the ground that sales at a high price should not be allowed to conceal dumped sales, was to treat export sales at a price above normal value (the price of the product in the exporter's home market, or his cost of production) as if they had been made at normal value. It is a method that makes discovery of dumping close to inevitable—the "export price" is an average of the prices of export sales that are *less* than normal value, and the normal value itself. That figure *cannot* be higher than normal value, and will typically be lower: if *any* export sales have been made at a price lower than normal value, dumping will be found.

This procedure was not expressly authorized before the Uruguay Round, though it was extensively used, especially by the European Union (the United States had its own averaging techniques). The agreement (Article 2.4.2), however, specifically authorizes it, albeit with what appear at first sight to be restrictions. It says that the averaging method described above may be used ". . . if the authorities find a pattern of export prices which differ substantially among different purchasers, regions or time periods and if an explanation is provided why such differences cannot be taken into account [by other means of averaging]."

If prices do not vary very much, however, use of this form of calculation will make little difference to the dumping margin. An antidumping authority bent on discovering high dumping margins will want to use it *only* when there is ". . . a pattern of export prices which differ substantially among different purchasers, regions or time periods." This "restriction" is a precondition for an antidumping authority to be able to inflate dumping margins by the means apparently restricted—it is not a restriction at all.

The severity of the requirement that national authorities must explain use of the method, moreover, obviously depends on the quality of explanation required; and the words of Article 17.6 quoted above cast doubt on the ability of a WTO panel to dismiss explanations on the basis of quality. "Authorization with restrictions," therefore, turns out to mean something very close to authorization *tout court*. It is not the only such case.

Another averaging practice inflates normal value by ignoring low-priced sales in the home market of the exporter on the ground that they are unprofitable, and therefore cannot be "in the ordinary course of trade." The effect is to raise the calculated normal value above a simple weighted average of prices in the exporter's home market.

Picking and choosing among transactions, however, may be more important as a means of inflating calculated profit margins. When costs are constructed, profit must be added to the cost of manufacture. An inflated profit margin therefore translates directly into an increase in the calculated dumping margin. Horlick and Shea (1995, 19–20) provide numerical examples to illustrate the effects of this practice.

Article 2.2.1 of the agreement authorizes the practice of picking and choosing (which the GATT had not done before), but it appears to restrict use of the practice by defining when it may be used: "Sales . . . may be treated as not being in the ordinary course of trade by reason of price and may be disregarded in determining normal value only if the authorities determine that such sales are made within an extended period of time [normally one year, but in no case less than six months] in substantial quantities [more than 20 percent of the volume sold] and are at prices which do not provide for the recovery of all costs in a reasonable period of time . . ." (the parenthetical inserts summarize the content of footnotes in the agreement).

The effect of these restrictions is not easily estimated by persons outside the process of determining dumping margins. An antidumping authority, though, may not find it very difficult to show that 20 percent of sales over a year are "sold at prices which do not allow recovery of all costs," especially in slump conditions, when antidumping is more intensively used. If so, the authorization plus restriction merely authorizes an intrinsically dubious practice.

Constructing Costs. Antidumping authorities often construct costs (that is, calculate them from accounting data). Some national authorities—notably those of the United States and the European Union—use different methods of construction for exports and home sales. Allowances for overheads or the advertising expenses of a related sales company on the home market of the exporter are sometimes limited and sometimes not given at all, even though such expenses are fully deducted on the export side of a calculation (Hindley 1988; Palmeter 1989). The costs of the exporter or the exporter's home-market price are thereby inflated, and, a dumping margin being the difference between these asymmetrically treated magnitudes, discovery of a dumping margin is facilitated.

The agreement deals with such practices in more detail and in firmer language than previous documents, and this firmer language presumably increases the probability that a panel addressing the issue will find asymmetric deductions to be inconsistent with the agreement.[6] The language of earlier attempts to control antidumping also seems clear, however—for example, that of the Tokyo Round Antidumping Code. Nevertheless, it failed to prevent the magnification of dumping margins by means of asymmetrical calculations.

Cumulation. Injury determination was discussed in chapter 2, but a further point is worth noting here. It is that, following the tactic of authorizing existing-but-not-expressly-authorized practices but placing restrictions on their use, Article 3.3 authorizes cumulation (that is, adding together the exports of several countries to determine the injury those exports have caused).

The conditions for cumulation follow:

1. The margin of dumping "in relation to each country is more than *de minimis*" (under Article 5.8, more than 2 percent).

2. The volume of imports from each country is not negligible [under Article 5.8, accounts for more than 3 percent of imports ". . . *unless countries which individually account for less than 3 percent of the imports . . . collectively account for more than 7 percent of imports . . .*" (emphasis added).

3. "A cumulative assessment of the effects of the imports is appropriate in the light of the conditions of com-

---

6. "Due allowance shall be made in each case, on its merits, for differences which affect price comparability, including differences in conditions and terms of sale, taxation, levels of trade, quantities, physical characteristics, and any other differences which are also demonstrated to affect price comparability" (Article 2.4). When the export price has been constructed, Article 2.4 requires that "if . . . price comparability has been affected, the authorities shall establish the normal value at a level of trade equivalent to the level of trade of the constructed export price, or make due allowance as warranted under this paragraph."

petition between imported products and the like domestic product."

What condition *3* means or might mean is obscure. Condition *1*, though, is consistent with tiny shares of imports in domestic sales. If imports account for 10 percent of sales, for example, 3 percent of imports represents a 0.3 percent market share! A charge that such a level of imports has caused injury to the domestic industry producing a like product is absurd on its face. Antidumpers, though, need not despair. So long as there are several exporting countries with tiny import shares, imports from them can be added together until a share of imports of 7 percent appears and makes it at least *more* plausible that imports have injured the domestic industry.

In an area in which bad economics and worse faith abound, this bids for some kind of prize. How can it possibly be justified—on the basis that exporters from a number of countries with a 1 percent market share between them are scheming together to force all other sellers out of the market with a *calculated* dumping margin of 2.01 percent?

Refund of Antidumping Duties—Duty as a Cost. Under the WTO, as formerly under the GATT, antidumping duties are supposed to be corrective, not punitive. They are refundable if dumping ceases.

The issue is not merely procedural. Retention of antidumping duties by national authorities places much heavier commercial cost on companies found to have dumped than a requirement, in effect, that they raise their prices. Nonrefund of duties therefore makes antidumping action a greater threat to exporters. It follows that threats of antidumping action will take a greater weight in any discussion of VERs or VER-like behavior between importers and exporters.

Article 9.3.2 of the agreement calls for the "prompt

refund, upon request, of any duty paid in excess of the margin of dumping. A refund of any such duty . . . shall normally take place within 12 months, and in no case more than 18 months, after the date on which a request for a refund, duly supported by evidence, has been made by an importer."

"Duly supported by evidence" is pregnant with possibilities of delay. Payment of interest on delayed reimbursements of dumping duties is not required.

In the European Union, marketing companies associated by ownership with the manufacturer of the product have found it especially difficult to obtain a refund. That is because the antidumping authority, when calculating the margin of dumping, deducts from the export price "any antidumping duties."

Thus, a product is found to have a dumping margin of 20 percent, and an antidumping duty of 20 percent is imposed upon it. The importer raises the price by 20 percent. On the methodology described in the last paragraph, however, dumping has not ceased. When the export price is constructed *after* imposition of the antidumping duty, that duty will be deducted. The 20 percent increase in the price of exports merely offsets the antidumping duty, so the antidumping authority will find an unchanged export price and an unchanged dumping margin. It will therefore not give a refund.

This has been a particular problem for exporters to the European Union who have been found to dump. The commission says that in this case,

> a reimbursement will be granted if the resale price [to an independent buyer] has been increased by an amount equivalent to the margin of dumping *and* the amount of duty paid [emphasis added].[7]

---

7. *Ball Bearings originating in Singapore (refunds)*, (*OJ* L148, 1988).

Article 9.3.3 of the agreement touches upon this issue, but with a notable lack of clarity:

> In determining whether and to what extent a reimbursement should be made when the export price is constructed in accordance with paragraph 3 of Article 2, authorities should take account of any change in normal value, any change of costs incurred between importation and resale, and any movement in the resale price which is duly reflected in subsequent selling prices, and should calculate the export price with no deduction for the amount of antidumping duties paid when conclusive evidence of the above is provided.

Alternatively stated, it appears that the authorities *may* calculate the export price with a deduction for the amount of antidumping duties paid when importers *fail* to provide *conclusive* proof of the above. "The above," however, includes "any movement in the resale price which is duly reflected in subsequent selling prices." It seems, therefore, that importers must conclusively prove not only that their price has increased by the amount of the dumping duty, but that the price charged *by those to whom they sell* has increased by that amount. Importers may have difficulty in conclusively proving this to skeptical authorities. If they fail to prove it conclusively, however, their export price may be calculated with deduction of dumping duties, as is EU practice. Other antidumping jurisdictions will be tempted to adopt this practice.

Outcome of the Round

The Uruguay Round has saddled the WTO with an antidumping agreement that is weak, judged against the pressures to which it will inevitably be subjected; and it has increased those pressures by banning VERs. Getting rid of

VERs was a laudable objective. The Uruguay Round settlement, though, runs the risk of merely transmuting VERs into corrupt antidumping actions.

That is not an improvement. The WTO risks association with sleaze and the cynicism that sleaze breeds. At worst, the WTO's loss of credibility will be so serious as to impair its effectiveness in other areas.

Antidumping in its present form has no proper purpose that cannot be better served by other means. Reform of the rules for application of antidumping can reduce the outrageous to the absurd and the absurd to the merely silly. But reform of the rules, the best the Uruguay Round could offer, cannot approach the fundamental issue, which is that antidumping itself has no sensible rationale. When a policy has no rationale, it is the policy itself, not the rules for applying it, that should be questioned.

5
What Can Be Done?

Current antidumping laws extend far beyond any rationale that might be found for antidumping. Without sensible justification, antidumping laws allow punitive responses to a range of importer activities and business tactics. That range, moreover, is continually expanding.

The multilateral trading system and the WTO are thereby threatened, and the execution of sensible trade policies by its member governments impeded. There is good ground for skepticism that the Uruguay Round Agreement will bring antidumping under control.

To bring antidumping under control again, WTO members must focus on the real problems in the area, and target WTO rules and national legislation on those problems. "Targeting" means that when the WTO authorizes antidumping, the authorization is subject to conditions that prevent application of antidumping in cases that display some similar symptoms, but are produced by behavior that is innocent or inoffensive.

Reform

The protectionist bent in antidumping law and policy has been aided by a habit of allowing "technical" matters to crowd out discussion of objectives. Legislators, trade negotiators, and antidumping authorities have found it less demanding to discuss *how* dumping margins ought to be calculated than to inquire *why* they should be calculated.

That they have sometimes arrived at strange conclusions is not surprising.

Predatory Dumping. The best case for action against dumping lies in the notion that the dumping may be predatory—that dumping may be designed to establish a monopoly by knocking out the competition. In industries with few sellers—but *only* in industries with few sellers—a case can be made for laws that permit action against predatory pricing.

An argument against such laws is that predatory pricing is unlikely to be an important real-world phenomenon. But that argues less *against* laws that permit action against predatory pricing than *for* access to such laws being conditional on the presentation of persuasive evidence that predatory pricing is in fact occurring or has occurred. The problem with current antidumping laws is not that they allow protection against predatory dumping—it is that in the name of such protection, they authorize action against a wide range of behavior that is not predatory, and in circumstances in which predatory dumping is inconceivable.

Accepting a case for powers to act against predatory dumping still leaves the question of *what* action. To restrict the application of current antidumping laws to industries in which predatory dumping is conceivable—that is, to industries with "small" numbers of producers at the global level, as suggested in chapter 2—would be a major advance even without further reform. Much more might be done, however.

The mere fact of dumping, even in an industry that is highly concentrated at the global level, is not evidence of *predatory* dumping. Whether differential-price or price-less-than-average-cost dumping is alleged, predatory dumping is very far from being the only possible explanation of it. A good antidumping law will separate unacceptable from acceptable behavior, as do domestic competition laws with respect to allegations of predatory pricing.

The fact that domestic competition laws deal with predatory pricing, however, prompts the question of why foreign sellers alleged to have engaged in predatory pricing should be treated differently from domestic sellers alleged to have engaged in predatory pricing. Only one answer seems to be available. It is that judgments against foreign sellers may be difficult and costly to enforce—sellers based in country A may have too few assets or persons within the grasp of country B law to allow enforcement of the decisions of B courts.

It seems unlikely, though, that a case for separating domestic and foreign predatory pricing can plausibly be made on the grounds of difficulties in enforcing domestic judgments on foreign parties. Difficulty in enforcing a competition-law judgment presumably implies that the offending seller has withdrawn from the market in which dumping occurred—otherwise the judgment could be enforced. It also implies that the seller will not return to the market—otherwise, enforcement of the judgment would once again be possible. To abandon a market to avoid competition-law penalties, though, would probably be uncommon. Modern exporters tend to sell many products. Abandoning the market would imply giving up sales of all of these: a move that is unlikely to make economic sense as a means of avoiding a competition-law judgment concerning one of them. Even if the predator did withdraw from the market, moreover, the problem of predatory pricing is solved even if the judgment cannot be enforced—not in the best way, which would entail the offending seller's giving up predatory tactics but not competition as such, but still, solved.

Predatory pricing should ideally be the subject of just one body of law, whether sellers alleged to have used that tactic are foreign or domestic. Competition law, which has a tradition of honestly trying to come to grips with the issues, is superior to antidumping law, which has no such tradition.

Industries with Large Numbers of Competitors. There is no good ground for antidumping action against the products of industries that contain many competitors. The antidumping agreement, however, authorizes action against industries containing very large numbers of sellers. Article 6.10 of the agreement, for example, says that:

> The authorities shall, as a rule, determine an individual margin of dumping for each known exporter . . . in cases where the number of exporters, producers, importers or types of product involved is so large as to make this impracticable, the authorities may limit their examination either to a reasonable number of interested parties or products by using samples which are statistically valid on the basis of information available to the authorities at the time of the selection.

Predatory pricing cannot justify action against sellers in such an industry. Indeed, the analysis of the earlier chapters yields only one circumstance in which there is a case for action against dumping in industries with large numbers of sellers—Viner's hypothesis of a cartel or arrangement that fixes the domestic price. As already noted, whatever the value of that hypothesis as an explanation of events in 1895, it does not seem likely to be valid in 1995; and it is likely to be invalid at either date for an industry containing the number of sellers visualized in the agreement. WTO authorization of antidumping action for industries with large numbers of sellers should be withdrawn. An exception could be allowed if the authorities of the importing country could provide evidence of a cartel or cartel-like organization fixing domestic prices in the exporting country.

To fail to find is not to prove that what is sought does not exist. There may be a case for action against dumping in industries with large numbers of sellers. If so, proponents of antidumping should make it.

Of course, the meaning of "large" is open to debate—though most will agree that if the number of sellers is so great that sampling is needed, that number is large. That debate, however, can await agreement on principle.

Differential-Price Dumping. In the discussion of fairness in chapter 2, a sanctuary market was noted as a necessary condition for differential-price dumping, and was also identified as the most obviously unfair of the circumstances surrounding such dumping. If sanctuary markets are at the center of the problem, common sense (as well as the theory of economic policy) suggests that sanctuary markets should be at the center of the solution.

Within the moral tradition of classical liberalism, sanctuary markets are indefensible. Antidumping as currently practiced, though, moves in the wrong direction—it makes a sanctuary market in country *A* an occasion for creating another sanctuary in country *B*, rather than removing the one in country *A*. Measures authorized by the WTO should aim at opening a sanctuary market, not permitting the creation of another one.

Some antisanctuary actions could in principle be negotiated in general terms. Governments might agree, for example, to allow duty-free importation of products originally exported from their countries.

In general, however, identification of the way in which a sanctuary market is maintained is a prerequisite for measures to remove it. An antidumping authority that claims to have discovered sustained differential-price dumping is implicitly claiming that a sanctuary market exists. An authority that claims to have identified a price difference could be required to produce an explicit statement of how the higher price in the home market of the exporter is maintained, supported by evidence. Failure to provide such an explanation would be a ground for rejecting the alleged price difference or any action based upon it.

When a satisfactory explanation is provided of how the difference is maintained, the priority should be to try to open the sanctuary market. Sanctuary markets often need the support of exporting-country governments, or, at least, their acquiescence in private-sector tactics to block imports. Identification of such actions or acquiescence provides a basis for talks between affected governments that aim at dismantling the blockage.

Sanctions against sanctuaries? What happens, though, if the means by which a higher price is maintained is identified, but negotiation fails to remove it? One possibility would be to authorize antidumping action: to permit closure or partial closure of the importing market if the exporting-country government refuses to open its country's market (or possibly maintains that it has no means of doing so).

Indeed, imposition of antidumping duties could be authorized as soon as:

- differential-price dumping has been verified
- the means by which the price difference is maintained have been satisfactorily identified

The ensuing negotiation would then be about removing the blockage to imports as a condition of removing antidumping duties. Pressure on the exporting industry and the exporting-country government would be increased if the product in question were produced in more than one country. Evidence regarding the way in which the price difference was maintained would be available to the governments of such countries, which would therefore be in a position to impose antidumping duties merely on a demonstration of differential-price dumping.

Price-Less-than-Average-Cost Dumping. The only threatening explanation of price-less-than-average-cost dumping is that the dumping is predatory. Once procedures are in place to deal with predatory dumping (which will certainly entail comparisons of the costs and prices of exporters), no further provisions for dealing with price-less-than-average-cost dumping are needed.

Concluding Comment

Some persons found in the vicinity of dead bodies may be murderers, and it is an aim of public policy to apprehend murderers. Nonetheless, a law that allowed the imprisonment of any person found in the vicinity of a dead body would be thought by most people to be a bad law. It might allow punishment of some guilty persons who would otherwise go free, but it would also subject many innocent persons to legal procedures and penalties that they had done nothing to merit.

Current antidumping law is justified by reference to the reasonable aims of public policy that it might serve. But it is a clumsy law. In the name of those reasonable aims, it authorizes action against practices that ought to be allowed.

If pursuit of reasonable aims made action against innocent practices inevitable, it might be necessary to consider whether the reasonable aims should be pursued at all. Current antidumping is so overextended—allows so many innocent practices to be attacked for so few proper policy aims—that dispassionate examination would likely lead to the conclusion that it should be abandoned.

But the reasonable aims of antidumping can be separated from action against innocent practices. The reasonable aims can be achieved—and better achieved—by relatively straightforward reforms. The resulting law would not look much like current antidumping law. But that is a virtue, not a problem.

References

Anderson, Simon P., Nicolas Schmitt, and Jean-Francois Thisse. 1995. "Who Benefits from Antidumping Legislation?" *Journal of International Economics,* vol. 38, pp. 321–37.

Appelbaum, H. M., and D. R. Grace. 1987. "U.S. Antitrust Law and Antidumping Actions under Title VII of the Trade Agreements Act of 1979." *Antitrust Law Journal,* vol. 56, pp. 497–518.

Areeda, P., and D. Turner. 1975. "Predatory Pricing and Related Practices under Section 2 of the Sherman Act." *Harvard Law Review,* vol. 88, pp. 697–733.

Barfield, Claude. 1994–1995. "Flat Panel Displays: A Second Look." *Issues in Science and Technology,* Winter, pp. 21–25.

Bastiat, Frédéric. 1854. *Pétition des fabricants de chandelles.* Guillaumin et Cie, Paris.

Blair, R. D., J. M. Fesmire, and R. E. Romano. 1991. "An Economic Analysis of Matsushita." *Antitrust Bulletin,* Summer, pp. 355–81.

Boltuck, R., and R. E. Litan, eds. 1991. *Down in the Dumps: Administration of the Unfair Trade Laws.* Washington, D.C.: Brookings Institution.

Bourgeois, Jacques, and Patrick A. Messerlin. 1994. *Competition and the EC Antidumping Regulations.* Collège Européen de Bruges and Institut d'Etudes Politiques de Paris, mimeo.

Brander, J., and P. Krugman. 1983. "A Reciprocal Dumping Model of International Trade." *Journal of International Economics,* pp. 313–21.

Bronckers, Marco C. E. J. 1995. "WTO Implementation in

the European Community—Antidumping, Safeguards, and Intellectual Property." *Journal of World Trade,* vol. 29, pp. 73–95.

Congress of the United States. 1994. *How the GATT Affects Antidumping and Countervailing Duty Policy.* Congressional Budget Office, Washington, D.C., September.

Dale, Richard. 1980. *Antidumping Law in a Liberal Trade Order.* Trade Policy Research Center, St. Martin's Press, New York.

Dixit, A. 1988. "Antidumping and Countervailing Duties under Oligopoly." *European Economic Review,* vol. 32, pp. 55–68.

EC Official Journal. 1989. C:150/3.

———. 1990. C:240/4.

Elzinga, K. E. 1989. "Collusive Predation: Matsushita v. Zenith." In J. E. Kwoka and L. J. White, eds. *The Antitrust Revolution.* Glenview, Ill.: Scott, Foresman, and Co., pp. 246–59.

Ethier, W. J. 1982. "Dumping." *Journal of Political Economy,* vol. 90, pp. 487–506.

Feinberg, R. M. 1989. "Exchange Rates and Unfair Trade." *Review of Economics and Statistics,* vol. 71, November, pp. 704–07.

Finger, J. M. ed. 1993. *Antidumping: How It Works and Who Gets Hurt.* Ann Arbor: University of Michigan Press.

Flamm, Kenneth S. 1994. "Flat-Panel Displays: Catalyzing a U.S. Industry." *Issues in Science and Technology,* Fall, pp. 27–32.

GATT. Agreement on the Implementation of Article VI of the General Agreement on Tariffs and Trade. Geneva, 1979.

Graafsma, F., and B. Driessen. 1994. "Commercial Defence Actions and Other International Trade Developments in the EC." *European Journal of International Law,* vol. 5, pp. 572–99.

Hart, Jeffrey A. 1993. "The Antidumping Petition of the Advanced Display Manufacturers of America: Origins and Consequences." *The World Economy*, vol. 16, January, pp. 85–110.

Hindley, B. 1988. "Dumping and the Far East Trade of the EC." *The World Economy*, December, pp. 445–63.

———. 1991. "Is There a Baby in the Bathwater?" In P. K. M. Tharakan, ed. *Policy Implications of Antidumping Measures*. Amsterdam: North-Holland, pp. 25–42.

Horlick, Gary N., and Eleanor C. Shea. 1995. "The World Trade Organization Antidumping Agreement." *Journal of World Trade*, vol. 29, pp. 5–31.

Joskow, P., and A. Klevorick. 1979. "A Framework for Analysing Predatory Pricing Policy." *Yale Law Journal*, vol. 89, pp. 213–70.

McGee, John. 1958. "Predatory Price Cutting: The Standard Oil (N.J.) Case." *Journal of Law and Economics*, vol. I, pp. 137–69.

———. 1980. "Predatory Pricing Revisited." *Journal of Law and Economics*, vol. 23, pp. 289–330.

Messerlin, P. A. 1989. "The EC Antidumping Regulations: A First Economic Appraisal." *Weltwirtshaftliches Archiv*, vol. 25, pp. 563–87.

Messerlin, P. A., and Y. Noguchi. 1991. *The EC Antidumping and Anticircumvention Regulations: The Photocopier Case*. Institut d'Etudes Politiques de Paris and Nomura Research Institute, Tokyo, mimeo.

Morkre, M. E., and K. H. Kelly. 1994. *Effects of Unfair Imports on Domestic Industries: U.S. Antidumping and Countervailing Duty Cases, 1980 to 1988*. Washington, D.C.: Bureau of Economics, Federal Trade Commission.

Palmeter, N. D. 1989. "The Capture of the Antidumping Law." *Yale Journal of International Law*, vol. 14.

———. 1991. "The Antidumping Law: A Legal and Administrative Nontariff Barrier." In R. Boltuck and R. E. Litan, eds. *Down in the Dumps: Administration of the Unfair Trade Laws*. Washington, D.C.: Brookings Institution.

———. 1995. "United States Implementation of the Uruguay Round Antidumping Code." *Journal of World Trade*, June, vol. 29, pp. 39–42.

Pangratis, Angelos, and Edwin Vermulst. 1994. "Injury in Antidumping Proceedings—The Need to Look Beyond the Uruguay Round Results." *Journal of World Trade*, vol. 28, pp. 61–96.

Prusa, Thomas J. 1992. "Why Are So Many Antidumping Petitions Withdrawn?" *Journal of International Economics*, vol. 33, pp. 333–54.

Shin, H. J. 1994. *Antidumping Law and Foreign Behavior: An Empirical Analysis*, Unpublished dissertation, Yale University.

Tirole, Jean. 1988. *The Theory of Industrial Organization*. Cambridge, Mass.: MIT Press.

U.S. Congressional Budget Office. 1994. *How the GATT Affects Antidumping and Countervailing Duty Policy*. Washington, D.C.: Government Printing Office.

U.S. International Trade Commission. 1991. *Certain High Information Content Flat Panel Displays and Display Glass Therefor from Japan*. Washington, D.C.: U.S. International Trade Commission.

———. 1995. *The Economic Effects of Antidumping and Countervailing Duty Orders and Suspension Agreements*. Washington D.C.: U.S. International Trade Commission, Publication 2900, p. 3-2.

Vermulst, J., and P. Waer. 1991. "The Calculation of the Injury Margin in EC Antidumping Proceedings." *Journal of World Trade*, December 1991, vol. 25, pp. 5–42.

———. 1995. "The Post-Uruguay Round EC Antidumping Regulation—After a Pit Stop, Back into the Race." *Journal of World Trade*, April 1995, vol. 29, pp. 53–76.

Viner, J. 1923. *Dumping: A Problem in International Trade*. Chicago: University of Chicago Press.

———. 1931. "Dumping." *Encyclopedia of the Social Science*, vol. 5. New York: Macmillan.

Weidemann, Rolf. 1990. "The Antidumping Policy of the European Communities." *Intereconomics*, January-February, vol. 25, pp. 28–35.

Willig, R. D. 1991. *Antidumping Policy: Protecting of Suppliers and Protecting of Competition*. Princeton University, mimeo.

About the Authors

BRIAN HINDLEY is reader in trade policy at the London School of Economics. He is a consultant on trade policy issues to a number of international organizations, and is codirector of the Trade Policy Unit of the London-based Centre for Policy Studies (CPS).

He published several articles in the *Trade Policy Review* of the CPS in 1994 and 1995. He is also a contributor to Jagdish Bhagwati and Robert E. Hudec's *Fair Trade and Harmonization* (1996).

Brian Hindley is British, but his A.B. and Ph.D. are both from the University of Chicago.

PATRICK A. MESSERLIN is professor of economics at the Institut d'Etudes Politiques de Paris. He is also consultant to the OECD and the EU Commission. From 1986 to 1990 he was a senior economist at the Research Department of the World Bank.

Mr. Messerlin has published many articles or reports on GATT-WTO issues, including antidumping, subsidies, services, and relationships between trade and competition policies, and on the trade policy of the European Community. He has coedited (with K. Sauvant) *The Uruguay Round: Services in the World Economy* (1990) and published *La nouvelle organisation mondiale du commerce* (1995).